HOPE & GLORY

A CATHOLIC INTRODUCTION TO THE BOOK OF REVELATION

Father Juan Alfaro, O.S.B.

D1115501

LIGUORI
PUBLICATIONS

One Liguori Drive
Liguori, MO 63057-9999
(314) 464-2500

Dedication

To Archbishop Patricio F. Flores, D.D.,
of San Antonio, Texas, on the Silver
Anniversary of his consecration

Imprimi Potest:
James Shea, C.SS.R.
Provincial, St. Louis Province
The Redemptorists

Bishop Paul Zipfel, V.G.
Auxiliary Bishop, Archdiocese of St. Louis

ISBN 0-89243-785-5
Library of Congress Catalog Card Number: 95-76230

Copyright © 1995, Liguori Publications
Printed in the United States of America
3 5 7 9 8 6 4 2
First Printing

This is a translation of *Esperanza y gloria: introducción al Apocalipsis
para católicos* (Liguori Publications, 1995).

Cover design by Christine Kraus

TABLE OF CONTENTS

Introduction

The wide acceptance by Hispanic readers in the United States and Latin America of my book *Preguntas y respuestas sobre la Biblia* inspired me to write this book about the concerns and questions that people have about the Book of Revelation.

At several biblical lectures I have given in Texas, California, Florida, New York, and Mexico, Revelation has been the participants' favorite topic. Recent events like the Gulf War and the Waco tragedy have prompted people to search for meaning in the Book of Revelation.

In the summers of 1987 and 1990, we offered courses on the Book of Revelation at the Mexican American Cultural Center in San Antonio, Texas, before record-setting crowds of inquiring minds. Many of the questions raised during those summer sessions are included in this book.

Today, the Book of Revelation has once again become one of the most read and studied books of the Bible. The reasons are social and cultural. The events portrayed in the book stir the imaginations of people facing an uncertain future.

The questions and answers have been arranged so as to provide an overall view of the book and its teachings.

1.

What is the Book of Revelation, and what exactly is "apocalyptic literature"?

The Book of Revelation is the last book of the Bible. Persons not well acquainted with the Bible may conclude that Revelation is unique both in style and content, unlike any other biblical book. In the Old Testament, however, we find an "apocalypse"—the Book of Daniel—that is written in apocalyptic style. Also, in the prophets, we find several short sections written in the same style: Isaiah 24-27; Ezekiel 40-48; Zechariah 9-14, and others.

In the New Testament, we can easily recall the apocalyptic descriptions of Jesus, the evangelists, and Paul, as they referred to the "end" of the world and the destruction of Jerusalem (see Mt 24-25; Mk 13; Lk 21; 1 Thes 2:1-12; 4:15-17; 2 Thes 2:1-12; 1 Cor 15:20-28; 2 Cor 5:1-5; 2 Pt 3:1-13).

In apocryphal literature (books not included in the inspired writings collections) we find many books of apocalyptic writings similar to the apocalyptic sections of the Bible: Enoch, Jubilee, Testament of the Twelve Patriarchs, Psalms of Solomon, the Assumption of Moses, Ezra IV, the books of Prophecies, Apocalypse of Baruch, Apocalypse of Paul, the Shepherd of Hermes, etc. These apocryphal books help us understand the apocalyptic sections of the Bible in the cultural context in which they were written.

The Book of Revelation and the apocalyptic literature is a way of thinking, a form of writing, a manner of viewing historical events: We are now in the final or eschatological period of time, and what is eternal has begun. The barrier between heaven and earth is being torn down as Christians experience firsthand the religious and social battle between good and evil, while beginning a new life in the celestial city; perseverance and faithfulness are guarantees of victory.

Apocalyptical narration makes use of imagery and categories from the Old Testament, especially those of the prophets and the Exodus. The apocalyptic books appear at a fixed point in time in the history of Israel and Christianity (from 200 B.C. to A.D. 200); they cover a period of suffering, persecutions, and calamities, where the forces of evil triumphed and human efforts to find liberation were ineffective or destined to fail.

It was in those difficult times that apocalyptic writers presented God as leader and savior; a source of promise and conviction for the future. Apocalyptic writers' dreams became messages of hope and salvation, and strengthened the will to survive, to resist evil, and to endure the hard times to come.

The author of Revelation stresses time and again that the triumph of the kingdom of God in history has been and forever will be manifest in the triumphant Christ. Christians had to dream of a new world order, especially so they could bear the oppressive "order" the Roman Empire imposed on different peoples. Revelation once again becomes a popular book for all levels of readers when they feel dispirited and downtrodden and are trying to build encouragement and confidence.

Apocalyptic books are frequently singled out for the authors' pessimistic view of history which they divide in two great eras or periods, the evil present and the ideal future. They describe great catastrophes that affect the entire universe and precede the beginning of the kingdom of God in the world; they narrate visions and revelations which support their writings; they tend toward ethical dualism, in which everything is either good or bad, black or white, with no half measures.

Apocalyptic writers narrate symbolic actions and accounts, and announce oracles and oracular warnings. Battles and mythical encounters frequently occur between the forces of good and evil, paralleling events and prophecies found in the Old Testament. In the view of apocalyptic authors, what happens on earth is many times a reflection of what happens in heaven.

Apocalyptic writings almost always are "anonymous," in that later writers try to mask themselves as famous writers of the past, as they "witness" events and "announce what is to come." That's why, when they describe what really happened before their time, these authors tend to be relatively accurate (even though their wording many times betrays them). But when these authors write about the present and the real future, they write in vague terms. The readers, who take for granted the writers' experiences, are thus impressed with the good news the writers announce for the future.

The author of the Book of Daniel, an early apocalyptic book, pretended to live in Babylon in 538 B.C. but actually wrote about 165-164 B.C. The author of Revelation probably wrote it around the year A.D. 95 but pretended to be writing during the time of Emperor Vespasian, around A.D. 75. As a result, the writer makes particular references to events surrounding the reigns of Vespasian, Titus, and Domitian (A.D. 69-95.) and circumstances that would be interpreted by readers to be "fulfilled" prophecies and predictions of future events.

2.

Why do English-speaking Catholics refer to the last book of the Bible as the Book of Revelation, while it's called Apocalypse in other parts of the world?

It's all a question of words and names. *Apocalypse* is a Greek word that signifies the removal of a veil or "revelation." The word *revelation* is a Latin term. The book begins with the word *Apocalypse* in keeping with the ancient tradition of using the first word or words of an untitled book for its heading. Today, many documents published by the Catholic Church (Vatican II, papal encyclical letters) use as titles

13

the beginning words of the written work: *Dei Verbum, Gaudium et Spes, Humanae Vitae,* and others.

The author of Revelation called his work "prophecy," but many specialists point out that the beginning and ending of the book are similar to the epistles or letters found in the New Testament.

The last book of the Bible has traditionally been known as the "Apocalypse" in Catholic circles. Recently, however, some non-Catholic groups have chosen to call the book "Revelation." This word is an exact translation of the Greek, *Apocalypse,* yet may mislead uninformed readers into believing that they will find in Revelation a separate and distinct revelation not found in any of the other books of the Bible. Many people mistakenly believe that they will find in this book the spectacular "revelations" that will signal the end of the world.

There is no problem in referring to this book by either name, although it is important that the reader not be misled into thinking that the book contains a revelation superior to the rest of the books of the New Testament.

The reader of the Apocalypse must bear in mind that the book is special not because it contains a wealth of "information" for the faithful, but because it contains especial challenges for everyday life. Its clear message is to challenge all Christians to remain faithful to the truths of their religion in the face of adversity and persecution, even through difficult and confusing times when everything appears to be going down. At the end of that dark tunnel a light awaits, the true light of victory with Christ.

The Roman Empire appeared to have supreme and irresistible powers. The emperors considered themselves gods and their empire divine. The author of Revelation wanted Christian readers to fear no power that enslaves people; to withstand the oppressor; to work to create a new order of esteem and fellowship among all peoples.

3

If the apostle John wrote the fourth gospel and the Book of Revelation, why are the two works so different?

Since the beginning of Christianity, people recognized the dissimilarities between the Book of Revelation and the fourth gospel. But a persistent tradition attibuted both works to the apostle John, the son of Zebedee. Later, at least one of the two works was attributed to the Beloved Disciple. The name "John" was common at that time, hence there could have been a source of confusion of names and persons.

At first, some Christians did not accept the inspiration of the Book of Revelation. It would be strange if the author of the book was an apostle and his doctrine was not recognized by some segments of the Church. In any case the author was well known in the Christian community and must have been an importante person since the Roman authorities eagerly sought his banishment.

Some Church Fathers believed that while the apostle John wrote the Book of Revelation, he was not the author of the fourth gospel. They believed the gospel according to John was written by John "the Presbyter," an important person who lived in the latter part of the first century and preached in the churches of Asia. This belief persisted until the sixteenth century.

In more recent times, experts believe that neither of the works was authored by John the Apostle. The author of the Book of Revelation appears to be coordinator of Christian communities and a brave and inspiring companion to his readers rather than a person in a position of authority. Some present-day writers attribute the Book of Revelation to other authors, such as John the Baptist or to one of his disciples, because of its presentation of Jesus as "the one who is to come." These are the same words that John the Baptist uses in the gospel when referring to Jesus (see Jn 1:27,30; Mt 3:11; 11,13; Rv 1:4,8).

Today, there is much talk about a "school," circle, sect, or community that was responsible for the theology of the two books attributed to John. The books may have been written by two very different individuals—although from the same school—whose works were separated by a span of twenty years; because of this they reflect clearly a change in the situation of the readers: the difficult period when Christians struggled for internal identity, and the period of the pressures derived from external persecution for their beliefs.

Revelation points out that the churches of Ephesus, Sardis, and Laodicea had lost their initial fervor, an indication that some time had passed since their conversion to Christianity. The Greek language used in Revelation is relatively poor, an indication that Greek was not the primary language of the author.

Even though the great differences between both books suggest they were not written by the same author, it is likely that the apostle John somehow was the inspiration for both, since they were written by people who probably were well acquainted with his beliefs.

It is rather strange that relevant terms in the fourth gospel are not found in Revelation: words such as *truth*, *eternal life*, *endure*, *darkness*, and *believe*. Still, both books carry the same Good News expressed in different ways.

The imagery and symbolism found in the fourth gospel are very similar to that used in Revelation, but the resemblance may not be perceived in a cursory reading of the works. Both books appear to have been written in the same surroundings, although parts of Revelation suggest the influence of Paul and the Ephesian community where his theology was well known.

Some have contrasted the eschatology of the fourth gospel with the eschatological perspective of the Book of Revelation, saying the fourth gospel proposes a realized eschatology (wisdom, salvation, and eternal life have come when the "hour" of Jesus arrived), while Revelation suggests an eschatology that would occur in the future. Notwithstanding, a careful reading of Revelation will show that the author is proposing an eschatology almost identical to that of the fourth gospel.

The Book of Revelation and the Gospel of John show great resemblance in their theology, and at times complement each other quite admirably; what one narrates theologically and "historically," the other narrates apocalyptically by means of symbols and imagery. An outstanding example of this complement is seen in the presentation of Calvary in the fourth gospel, and the vision of the Woman and the Dragon in Revelation.

The gospel is centered in the "life" and personal characteristics of Jesus as a model of the personality of the believer, while Revelation is centered in the glorious and triumphant figure of Jesus as a model and source of hope for the believer.

4.

Why is the Book of Revelation so different from the other books of the Bible?

Revelation is distinguished from other books of the Bible more for its literary style than for its doctrinal content. More than half of the 404 verses contained in Revelation allude to texts, images, or figures of the Old Testament. It could be said that the author has created a "new mosaic" with tiny stones from many old mosaics.

In Revelation there is only one direct reference to an Old Testament text (13:3). That reference, however, is not an exact citation, but is itself a composition of various texts. Some have come to view Revelation as a Christian interpretation of the Old Testament. It should be said that the Book of Revelation is an interpretation of the New Testament to solve the contemporary problems of a developing Church.

The author of Revelation alludes to several basic themes contained in the New Testament, writing in symbolic, yet, tangible language what the eschatological sermons of the synoptic Gospels presented in general and abstract form (see Mk 12; Lk 21). The books most quoted or alluded to in Revelation are Exodus, Ezekiel, Zechariah, Daniel, Genesis, Deuteronomy, Numbers, Psalms, Amos, and Isaiah. Among the contacts of Revelation with the rest of the Bible, the following are the most important:

a) Prophetic call, mission, and visions: generally the author is inspired by Isaiah 6, Jeremiah 1, and Ezekiel 5-20. The visions of the seven seals, together with the calamity they provoke, seem to explain the sermon of the thirteenth chapter of Mark and its synoptic parallels. The vision of the trumpets is closely related to Exodus. Prophet Zechariah provides the substance for the visions of the four horsemen, the harlot, and the horns. The vision of the scroll (Rv 10:8-11) is inspired by Ezekiel (3:1-13).

b) The seven letters to the churches: in form and content, they are apocalyptic oracles that resemble the oracles of the prophets.

c) The punishments and the plagues: generally, they are inspired by the plagues of Egypt (Ex 7-10), in the destruction of Sodom and Gomorrah (Gn 18-19), and in the fall of Babylon (Is 13).

d) Beatitudes and curses: they are inspired by the benedictions and maledictions in Deuteronomy (28), and also in Psalms and Proverbs.

e) The liturgical elements: the temple, altar, tabernacle, trumpets, smoke, fire, incense, and thunder are generally taken from the Book of Exodus.

5

Why is the Book of Revelation such an intriguing book?

Many people consider Revelation an especially intriguing book because they see it as a "prophecy" of terrible and spectacular events that will occur in the near future, are happening now, or, in part, have come to pass.

Others see Revelation as a puzzle whose key has been hidden for 2000 years and is just now being deciphered. To make matters worse, these same people believe that they are the only ones who hold the "mysterious" key to the book. Still others call Revelation the "book of the seven seals" and consider the work impossible to decipher.

Revelation certainly is a book that defies the imagination. Because of this, some refuse to read it or pay much attention to it. Others, however, delight in exercising their imagination as they attempt to satisfy their curiosity by foretelling future events in our history.

A good number of present-day evangelical preachers, especially those who work in television, glory in their imaginative interpretations of the Book of Revelation—at times allowing their imaginations to run completely wild—disregarding the rest of the Bible, common sense, or the course of history. These preachers play on the ignorance of people and exploit the "love of fear" mentality that exists in our culture. While some people like to watch scary movies, others prefer to listen to these preachers' scary predictions, convinced that prophecies of harm will not affect them personally, but will hurt those "villains" who are not part of their evangelical groups. Listeners like to hear of bad things that will happen to "the others" but not to them.

Various religious groups (Jehovah's Witnesses, Adventists) have repeatedly tried to calculate when the end of the world will occur. They have been mistaken each time, and each

19

time they have had to adjust their calculations. However, even during the times of Paul, there were Christian agitators who believed the end of the world was imminent. But, Paul insistently corrected them (see 2 Thes 2:1-3). It is important to keep in mind that Jesus did not come to reveal for us the *end* of the world, but the *finality* of the world according to God's plan. Revelation—like most of the prophetic books—looks at the present more than to the future; a present that needs to be changed; a time to fight for justice and liberty of the oppressed in order to create a better future and a new world.

The apocalyptic books, in general, were difficult to understand for the authors' contemporaries. Consequently, only the Book of Daniel was accepted among the Jewish writings of the Old Testament, and only the Book of Revelation of John among the Christian writings of the New Testament. These books were written for select communities that were, to a certain extent, isolated from the general cultural current, and other covenant writings of the period. Among the manuscripts found at Qumran, an Essene community west of the Dead Sea, eight copies of the Book of Daniel have been discovered. This would indicate that the work of Daniel was very important to that desert community.

Revelation was written during a period when the newborn Church was experiencing the bloody persecutions of the Roman Empire. The author alludes to events that were occurring in his time and that Christian readers knew well. Because of this, the readers accepted his message, allowing for the fact that the author spoke more from his heart than from his mind.

The persecutions of Christians are part of God's plan. Christians are called to fight to change a world clinging to self-interests and sin. Sinners will fight back, but Christians have nothing to fear, for good will triumph over evil with the power of God.

In the end, the Book of Revelation sought to encourage Christian readers to stay strong and resist the powers of the

Roman Empire. If the book fell into the hands of the persecutors, the symbolic style of writing would mask the subversive intent of the message. For us, it would be interesting to identify present leaders who have inherited the evil agenda of the first persecutors of the Church.

We should recall that John directly opposed the empire that proclaimed the emperor a god and gave him other blasphemous titles. The empire exploited and crushed nations in the name of a false god. Christians, sooner or later, would have to declare themselves mortal enemies of such an imperial system. As the opposition mounted, the Roman Empire, which had tolerated all forms of religious beliefs of conquered nations, became unyielding and cruel with Christianity. The new religion attacked the "divine" rights of the empire, and attempted to create a new society. The Christian communities were the model for the future of the new society that was to be created.

6.

If the Book of Revelation is a "prophecy," what does it prophesy?

The above question appears to imply or reflect what is expressed by television preachers and evangelists who dream up predictions of the future and who like to present their personal "religious" view of history. This point of view generally teaches *dispensationalism*, a theory which divides the history of humanity into seven stages, eras, or "dispensations," through which the providence of God has guided humanity since the time of creation.

The Book of Revelation is of special importance to dispensationalists. According to them, it speaks exclusively of what will happen in the future. For these teachers, the author of Revelation was a sort of fortuneteller who predicted events far into the future.

Dispensationalism is especially attractive to those with

21

superficial religious knowledge. To them, the division of the history of salvation into seven stages may appear scientific and well thought out. At a critical level, however, such a view will end up being a simple and very poor division of sacred history, reflecting a serious lack of biblical knowledge. There are more and better ways to present and divide biblical history (as can be seen in many Bible study manuals), and anyone with a little knowledge of the Bible can do it better than the old dispensationalist system.

Dispensationalism as a "modern system" was introduced by John Nelson Darby (1800-1882) in England. From the beginning, it was attractive more for its simplicity than for its compatibility with historical reality. According to dispensationalism, the history of salvation, from the beginning of the world to its consummation, passes through seven stages or dispensations. The common names for these periods are

1. **Innocence:** The period of paradise with Adam and Eve until original sin
2. **Conscience:** Humanity after paradise
3. **Human government:** People dominate one another and begin to dominate nature (the Flood and the Tower of Babel)
4. **Promise:** Abraham and the Patriarchs
5. **The Law:** From the covenant of God with his People on Mount Sinai until the death of Christ
6. **The Church:** from the Resurrection of Jesus to the present
7. **The kingdom:** the millennium: a soon-to-come period of joy and victory for God's faithful. During this epoch all the promises described in the Old Testament will be fulfilled.

Catholics, like other Christians, believe that Jesus has already brought about the completion of all prophecies and promises, and that the whole Old Testament was, as Paul teaches us, the actual period of promise, not just the era of patriarchs. The first three stages of fundamentalist doctrine are quite arbitrary. Moreover, the kingdom of God has already arrived and has been with us ever since Jesus began his mission, and especially since his death on the cross—a death that brought us eternal liberation.

We should bear in mind, in opposition to the dispensationalists, that there is no interruption in the periods covering the promise, the Law, and the Church; instead, a continuity of revelation exists, which binds the stages. God, who had spoken through the patriarchs and prophets in the Old Testament, finally spoke through his Son. Biblical truth has been given to us to challenge our way of living and to call us to a profound conversion, not to occupy our minds with imaginary calculations and visions.

As "prophecy," the Book of Revelation affirms a faith and a way of believing in God in the midst of certain concrete circumstances of life. The author of Revelation wanted to affirm God's supremacy against the Roman supremacy, the grandeur of the Christian communities versus the greatness of Roman life and civilization. The Roman world was destined to fail. The future was in the hands of Christians and their way of living.

7.

What is the best method
for studying the Book of Revelation?

For a personal and individual study of Revelation, I would not recommend a method other than one used to study, read, or meditate over other books of the Bible. References to the Old Testament have to be verified, along with parallel texts that refer to concrete themes of Revelation. In addition, one must find the meaning of those texts in the light of the gospels and the rest of the New Testament, or how a specific doctrine, such as the teaching of the "end" of the world, appears in the gospels.

To learn more from reading and study, one must carefully read the introductions to each book, along with the notes that explain the difficult verses. It is important to consult authoritative reference sources or, more specifically, Catholic authors who specialize in holy Scripture. In any case, it is better to study with a formal Bible-study group, particularly when analyzing the Book of Revelation, to avoid inflamed and exaggerated interpretations.

For the benefit of the study group, there are several approaches to encourage active participation and ensure meaningful dialogue:

a) Members of the study group can try to picture the apocalyptic imagery, sketching it in bright colors. Participants should feel free to add details and dimensions to one another's work. Students can then be asked to explain their drawings, using their imagination and creativity to describe their representations. The imagery should be viewed first as a whole and then focus on its details.

b) Read the texts out loud in a rhetorical tone of voice. Hymns and acclamations should be read in a group. Afterward, each member of the group can outline their impressions and point out parts of the text containing special challenges, not only for them but for all Christians.

c) Dramatize descriptions of visionary events and celestial liturgies. Use body motions and gestures.

d) Listen to dramatic music that relates to accounts in the text, for example, Revelation 11:19.

e) Examine and analyze artists' paintings on themes from the Book of Revelation.

There is no easy way to study any book of the holy Scripture, as all the books come from a culture very distant from ours. The application of the texts to our way of living, and the attempt to identify with the original readers can help us see new dimensions. But it is important to always read and study works written by experts and authoritative sources in the field.

8.

What things must be taken into account to better understand the Book of Revelation?

In the first place, it is important to remind readers that the author refers to the Book of Revelation as "prophecy" (see Rv 1:3; 10:7; 11:18; 22:6,9,18). It is not a book of secret revelations, but a prophecy that denounces human exploitation and oppression, especially those that take on a religious dimension. Revelation calls for a personal conversion and change in the existing order: the "beast" and its institutions must be brought down.

From the beginning, Revelation was difficult to interpret because of the unusual imagery, symbolism, and message. We are twenty centuries away from an author who wrote in a symbolic language, presumably known only to readers in certain churches of Asia. For this reason, readers should familiarize themselves with biblical symbolism in general before beginning a study of Revelation. Readers need to use their imaginations since the author uses repeatedly expressions such as *like* (characteristic of) as in, "...a sea of glass *like* crystal," and *like* (similar to) as in, "...heard a voice *like* a trumpet." These descriptions should not be taken literally but rather, as the author intended, from a symbolic perspective, especially when reality is cloaked in mysterious garments.

The reader should also bear in mind that the writings of Revelation many times present a preview of events that will occur or will be described in detail in other parts of the book. This could be compared to a television program that opens with a general view of a large area, and then focuses on a

25

small section of that area. Thus, chapter twelve of Revelation generalizes events and accounts that will be narrated in detail throughout the rest of the book. The text of Revelation 11:19 prepares for 15:5-7; 14:6-12 introduces what will be described in 15:1-16:21. Revelation 16:19 refers to 17:1-19; 17:14 announces the text of 19:11-16, and so on.

It is important to understand the problems and circumstances of the churches for whom the author was writing. It was difficult for Christians to see the hand of God in the persecutions of their communities by Roman authorities who saw themselves as truly omnipotent and eternal. A famous German author once said that the Book of Revelation is a book of its time, written in its time and for its time, and not for distant generations. Understanding the history of the first century will help clarify many obscure points of Revelation.

Revelation was probably written during the reign of the Roman emperor Domitian, near the end of the first century. Its significance, however, like the gospels and the letters of Paul, is valid for all time. It is a prophetic book because it is a parable of history with valuable significance for all centuries. The author alludes to events of his time interpreting them through his visionary experiences.

What the reader learns from the text will depend on the questions that are asked from the text. This applies, of course, to all biblical books. As a parallel, to know a person well does not depend as much on the time spent together, as in the kind of dialogue and conversation shared with that person. It's possible to live with someone for many years without really knowing that person. When reading Revelation, or any biblical text, there are three key questions that must be asked about the text:

1.) What does the text really say?
2.) What did the text mean for the author's contemporaries?

3.) What does it mean for us today, and how are we challenged by it?

The Book of Revelation, with its art and symbolism, has been better understood by artists than theologians. Painters, such as Dali, and musicians like Handel succeeded in capturing the true spirit of the book. A bit of imagination and an artistic vein will help to better understand this book.

9.

What is the official doctrine of the Catholic Church regarding the Book of Revelation?

There are no special doctrines of the Catholic Church that directly address the Book of Revelation; in fact, the Church considers the study and interpretation of the gospels much more important. Above all, the Church asks that common sense be used.

During the first centuries of the Church, some Christians had a difficult time accepting the Book of Revelation as equal to the other books of the New Testament. For example, the Muratorian text, written during the second century, is specific about the inspired nature of the books that were judged acceptable to the Church: "We will accept only the Apocalypse of John and of Peter, even though some among us refuse to read them in church" (adapted). It is important to note that in some early lists of the Canon of the New Testament, the Book of Revelation is not mentioned: the Catechesis of Cyril of Jerusalem of A.D. 348; the Council of Laodicea of A.D. 360; and others.

In the fourth chapter of the decrees of the Fourth Council of Toledo A.D. 633, the following is prescribed: "The Apocalypse should be accepted as a divine book since it is backed by the authority of many councils, and by the decrees of the holy Synods of Rome that attribute the work to the evangelist Saint John.... Henceforth, if anyone refuses to accept it, or does not preach it in Mass during the period from Easter to Pentecost, that person shall be subject to excommunication" (adapted).

In the Middle Ages, during the thirteenth and fourteenth centuries, historic interpretations, such as those of Joaquim de Fiore (+1202) and Nicholas of Lira (+1340), were condemned because of their opinions on the Book of Revelation; they said Revelation prophesied seven distinct periods in the history of the Church. Like some modern readers, they saw only direct and exclusive allusions to events occurring in their times, without considering the nature of biblical prophecy or the literary dimensions of the apocalyptic style.

Millenarianism—the so-called thousand-year reign of Christ on earth among the chosen, especially martyrs—has encountered opposition from the Catholic Church since ancient times. The doctrine is a modification of the Jewish belief in a chosen nation that will come to rule over all nations and govern the world. The millennium also was proposed in various forms by a few of the Church Fathers (Justin, Irenaeus, Hippolytus).

Millenarianism was officially condemned at the third ecumenical Council of Ephesus in A.D. 431. In the twentieth century, millenarianism has once again lifted its head in many Protestant circles and in several Catholic groups. The Holy Office—the Roman Congregation that protects the purity of the Faith—officially declared that millenarianism can be dangerous and, while not directly condemning it, said: "In recent times, the Sacred Congregation of the Holy Office has been asked more than once to comment on millenarianism, which teaches that Christ will come to reign on earth before the Final Judgment."

"Having examined this subject in the plenary session of Wednesday, July 19, 1944, the most eminent Cardinals charged with protecting the purity of the Faith, after listening to the opinions of their consultants, decreed as follows:

The system of a mitigated millenarianism cannot be taught without some risks" (adapted).

The Church wants the study of Revelation to be approached with care and common sense; to take into account the teachings of the Fathers of the Church, the analogy of the faith (in the Bible there are no contradictions in matters of faith because God is the author), and in the grand biblical context. It is important, more in this book than in others, to consider the literary genre and symbolism used by the author.

The Book of Revelation should be seen in relationship to the rest of Christian revelation, and not as if it were a separate and exotic book. Its interpretation and symbolism should be done with consideration to the symbolism in the other books of the Bible, especially that of the prophets and Exodus.

10.

Were the Apocalyptic visions of John real or imagined? Where did he get his images?

It could be said that John had but one vision—that of a Christian way of life in a hostile world. Like the prophets of the Old Testament, John was a man of vision much more than a man of visions; much the same as the prophetic teachers, he used symbolic actions and prophetic oracles to communicate his teachings.

Obviously, John didn't spend a weekend watching a kind of movie in the sky which later he described in all its details; he wrote the "script of the movie" by reshaping many elements taken from the Old Testament. Fundamentalists have no problem in imagining such a spectacular vision, since their credulity appears to have no limits.

John wrote Revelation using the same technique practiced by other apocalyptic writers who wrote on a desk while searching and refining biblical images, and using their imagination to adapt them to the critical situation they were writing about. It is important to remember that John wrote in Revelation something he had lived—things that happened in the life of the Church. John described for us in Revelation his experience of the victory of Christ in the life of Christians and throughout history, especially during the times of tension and discrimination caused by the Roman persecutors.

John described the persecutions of Christians in light of the experiences of God's People in the Old Testament. John took the imagery of the Old Testament and gave it a new life and purpose, since the New Covenant comes to broaden and perfect the old. The God who saved his oppressed people in the Old Testament is coming to save his People in the New Testament. The future of all Christians is victory and liberation.

11.

What is the symbolic meaning of the numbers that appear in the Book of Revelation?

Revelation frequently makes use of numerology, since numbers had great significance for the author's contemporaries. Some numbers were considered good, while others were unlucky (much like the number 13 today).

Jews believed that numerical symbols held secret values and developed a system called *Gematria*, almost to a science, for their use of numbers to interpret the Bible. The principal numbers used in Revelation, with their symbolic meanings, are the following:

3 - (thirty-one times) like number seven, denotes greatness, superlative

$3^1/_2$ - half of seven, indicates imperfection, brevity, failure, time of trial or persecution. Three and one-half years is the duration of the tribulations following the uprising of the Maccabees from 168 B.C. to 165 B.C.

4 - (twenty-nine times) - the four cardinal points; world; universality

6 - seven minus one, symbolizes imperfection and failure

7 - (forty-three times) - plenitude, perfection, fullness, totality

10 - complete number; perfection

12 - (twenty-two times) three times four, eschatological perfection, twelve tribes of Israel, God's People

24 - two times twelve, plenitude of God's People in the Church

42 - number of months in three and one-half years, the significance of which is related to the number $3\frac{1}{2}$

666 - "seven minus one" three times denotes imperfection and total failure

777 - three sevens represent perfection and absolute plenitude

1,000 - multitude; large quantity; innumerable quantity

1,260 - number of days in three and one-half years; time of tribulation and trials

12,000 - limitless number; members of the old People of God

144,000 - twelve squared multiplied by one thousand; limitless and complete number symbolizing the members of the new People of God

What are some other important symbols in the Book of Revelation?

Apocalyptic authors used symbols to communicate ideas and feelings. There are some spiritual experiences that are difficult to describe in terms of other experiences and human realities; hence the use of descriptive images. Christian writers of mysticism frequently used this style. The ancient Aztecs gave meaning to their divine sentiments by associating them with images of flowers and songs, known as *Floricanto*.

The author of Revelation created a generous mix of colors, sounds, and objects, producing elaborate imagery impossible to visualize concretely and physically. The details of a vision should not be seen in isolation. John wanted in some way to present to us the unimaginable, to give us an idea of the divine greatness.

Following the tradition of apocalyptic writers, the author of Revelation made special use of colors, objects, and symbolic animals:

Colors:
>   **White** - victory, glory, joy, purity
>   **Red** - blood, violence, homicide, vengeance
>   **Black** - death, impiety, harm
>   **Green** - death, decomposing cadaver, pestilence
>   **Purple** - luxury, royal splendor
>   **Blue** - purity, transparency, color of sea, color of sky

Objects:
>   **Belt** - royalty, priesthood
>   **Full-length robe** - priesthood
>   **Crown** - royalty, power, victory

Palm - victory

Star - angel, power, community leader

Sword - war, judgment

Trumpet - alarm, message, call to attention, liturgy

Gaze - judgment

Eyes - wisdom, knowledge

Horns - strength, power

Wings - mobility, protection

Seals - secret, importance, belonging

Candlestick - the community, Israel

Gold - quality, preciousness, value

Precious stones - luxury, wealth, beauty

Grey hair - wisdom, eternity

Babylon - city oppressing the People of God

New Jerusalem - new Zion, new People of God

Living creatures:

Angels - messengers of God, personification of God and natural forces

Horses - military might, invasion, speed

Woman - symbol of a nation (Jewish, pagan, church)

Lamb - salvation, simplicity, humility, sacrifice of Jesus, Day of the Lord

Beast - the Roman Empire, the emperor

Dragon - serpent, Satan

Lion - bravery, cruelty, king of wild animals

Bear - cruelty, strength

Eagle - liberty, far reaching, queen of birds

Bull - fortitude, king of domestic animals

13.

Does the Book of Revelation speak of historic events or is the book an announcement of things to come when the world ends?

The author of Revelation, as we said, called his book "prophecy." Like all prophecies, and like the gospels and Bible in general, Revelation has a message for all times. It is a standard or mirror of events in our past and present. Biblical prophecy is not just an announcement of the future but a declaration of faith in God's continuous action; a prophetic call for the conversion of people, while bringing salvation and liberation to oppressed peoples.

A prophecy, even if it weren't "fulfilled" in the future, would still be true as an affirmation of faith. When God announces punishment, he is seeking not to punish but to convert; if people listen to the message and change their ways, no punishment will be inflicted upon them. The prophetic announcement, in this case, would have "fulfilled" its purpose in exhorting the faithful to convert; thus, the predicted punishment, secondary to the announcement, would not occur.

However, as is the case in prophetic messages, the author of Revelation was writing directly for the readers of his time and not for the future. He wanted to give them hope to endure hardships and persecutions. Christians could not reconcile their differences with the oppressive Roman Empire and had to offer resistance—with hope for a triumphant ending, with the help of God. As we said, Revelation is a book written "in its time, from its time, and for its time."

We should dismiss the presumption that we are close to the end of the world, and that the events of the Book of Revelation are only now taking place. In biblical thinking, the end of the world came with Christ's victory on Calvary.

The war between good and evil was decided right then and there, although battles are still being fought. The devil and the forces of evil are going down to defeat, yet remain capable of inflicting harm on the careless and unprepared. (An example of our time that can help us understand is the famous D-Day invasion of Normandy, France, during the second World War. The war was lost on the beaches; the Germans could not prevent the allied landings nor impede the advance of armies who would fight until total victory was achieved.)

Some evangelicals erroneously believe that for centuries Revelation was incorrectly interpreted by people who were convinced that theirs were the final days. These persons believe that only today, at the end of the twentieth century, can we correctly interpret the book because we are truly in the world's final days.

We must bear in mind that when biblical authors mentioned the "last days," they were not referring to chronological time, but to religious and theological time periods. It is a "quality" or kind of time we live in. Since the coming of Jesus, we live in a time of special urgency and vigilance, a time of salvation and liberation full of opportunities and challenges for the believer because the revelation of God is always at the door of our life. The last word of God—the final word of unconditional love and forgiveness—was given to us through his Son on Calvary. It was there that God's love until the end was revealed for us.

Revelation is, as a prophecy, a book for all times. Every time a person reads Revelation and feels challenged to convert, to struggle and persevere, Revelation is being "fulfilled"; or rather, is fulfilling its final purpose to elicit response from readers.

Revelation, like other apocalyptic writings in the Bible, speaks not of the end of the world, but of the finality or purpose of the world. The world will not come to a stop in a grinding collision with a fixed object. It has a destiny which

God directs throughout history. Revelation reveals not the end, but the purpose of history since Christ's victory on Calvary.

God wants to create a new city, the City of God, the New Jerusalem, with which to reach the goal of the first creation. It's up to us, inspired by the Book of Revelation and the rest of the Bible, to work to make the City of God a reality for us as we struggle against the beast and totalitarianism that periodically raise their heads through history. At the end of the book, Revelation describes for us in beautiful poetic strokes, the peace, brotherhood, and justice that reign in the new City of God.

Revelation gives us an idea of the obstacles that will have to be overcome in the process of constructing a city and a new world, but assures us of success.

One must remember that although Jesus did not become a zealot, he did not condemn this group. Paul counseled respect for authority because Christianity was not intended to be an alternative political force. However, Christianity must always be a critical and prophetic movement called to denounce those in power who resort to repression.

14.

How does the Book of Revelation relate to our own history?

Revelation encompasses all of history, not just a particular period or moment in time. It is a book about what took place, what is taking place now, and what will take place in the future. Revelation presents Christ as the key to understanding and judging history.

John wrote during difficult times when history appeared to make no sense. Christians lived under an empire that considered itself divine. Although solid in appearance, it was actually made of soft clay from top to bottom.

The empire imposed its oppressive laws over nations and

appeared to triumph over the new born Church—often by killing Christians. It was in that situation that John realized that Jesus' sacrifice could give meaning to his life. He also realized that through sacrifice, one can actually control history. The person who does not fear death but is willing to make the ultimate sacrifice is assured of victory.

The history of mankind does not depend on the decisions of the rich and powerful, but on the decisions of God. Heaven and earth are in close communion, and the events in one caused repercussions in the other. Christians who know and embrace God's decisions are the true guides of history.

God wants history to follow its course to the end, creating a new humanity and establishing profound human relations based on the values of the gospel. To accomplish this, God relies on Christians to cooperate and carry out his mission. History marches toward the liberation of the Sons of God from the days of the Exodus, across the defeat of Babylon and the fall of Rome, to a celestial Jerusalem on earth. John described this in the events of the first century. It is now up to us to discover the course of God's history in our own century, reading the signs of our times.

15.

Does the first vision in the Book of Revelation hold a special significance? (1:9-20)

In many ways, the opening vision in Revelation serves as an introduction to the entire book. It introduces us to the symbolism that unfolds throughout the book. It presents Jesus as the Lord of glory and history, as it will appear in each chapter. From the very beginning we are told that the triumph of Jesus is assurance of victory for all his followers.

In the introduction (Rv 1:13), Jesus is described as "Son of Man," whom Daniel in his prophecy describes as "coming with the clouds of heaven" (7:13). The initial vision is an indication that the book will deal with the "Final" Judgment of the world.

Jesus is identified by seven titles, in order, which describe his personality and work on behalf of Christians:

1. Jesus the Messiah.
2. The Faithful Witness.
3. The Firstborn of the dead.
4. The Ruler of the kings of the earth (see Rv 19:16).
5. The One who loves us.
6. The One who freed us from our sins by his blood.
7. The One who has made us into a kingdom of priests for his God and Father.

The first vision also describes, with echoes of Exodus 19:16, the grandeur and sublimity of Christ, with characteristics similar to those of "the Ancient One" (Dan 7:13-14). The human-divine figure was like a Son of Man, wearing an ankle-length robe (he was a priest), with a gold sash around his chest (like the kings); the hair of his head was white as wool or snow (a sign of old age or eternity and wisdom).

His eyes were like a fiery flame (penetrating; they saw and knew everything); his feet were like polished brass refined in a furnace (firmness, stability and security); his voice was like the sound of rushing water (that the whole world could hear and whose power caused fear).

In his right hand he held seven stars (he held the destiny of the seven communities and the powers of the universe; he was the Lord of glory and history); a sharp two-edged sword came out of his mouth (like the categorical life-or-death sentence of a judge); his face shone like the sun at its brightest (like the face of Jesus at the Transfiguration), a Christ glorious and irresistible.

Christ appears in the midst of seven lamp stands, which are thought to be related to the great menorah or seven-branched lamp stand, similar to the one in the Temple of

Jerusalem. It stood for the People of God in the Old Testament; in this case, however, the lamp stand is symbolic of the new People of God, the Church. Christ is in the midst of the seven churches, which the author will address next. Christians can place their full trust in Jesus because from the beginning he has revealed himself to us as One who is all-powerful in heaven and on earth.

In each of the letters to the churches, John repeats the titles he assigned to Jesus in this first vision, and then adapts them to the spiritual conditions of each church.

16.

What is so special about the seven churches in the Book of Revelation?

The seven churches in the Book of Revelation were like many other churches of their time. They were not exceptional communities with special problems, but simple churches for which the author felt a certain responsibility.

The seven communities of the churches were linked by a circular road guarded by Roman soldiers. Some have suggested that the author was referring to the seven principal cities of the region, though this may not be entirely true since there were other important cities close by, such as Hierapolis and Colosas, which had notable Christian communities.

Some authors see the seven churches (the number "seven" symbolizing plenitude) as seven communities representing all facets of the universal Church. The problems facing these churches were the same problems plaguing all churches because every local church, while retaining its individuality, is an embodiment of the universal Church. The number "seven" signifies perfection and totality. In these churches other authors have tried to see—despite their lack of critical foundation—some kind of oracles that announce the stages and problems the universal Church will encounter throughout its long history.

The seven churches faced the problems of Christian subjects of the Roman Empire, including the pressure created by the religious and social demands of the imperial cult. Almost all of the cities mentioned were important centers of imperial worship.

Some Christians could have been easily influenced by false teachers who promoted or favored an accommodation to pagan customs and practices. Others may have been deceived by the imperial propaganda that depicted the Roman power as the benefactor of humanity, while hiding the imperialist dimension of methodical and ruthless oppression and exploitation. This would have created doubts, problems, and divisions in the bosom of the Christian community. Also, some of these churches suffered the persecutions instigated by Jews who were jealous over the progress of the new religion.

17.

What was the aim of the author when he wrote the letters to the seven churches?

The letters written to the seven churches of the Book of Revelation are a type of apocalyptic oracle, written in symbolic language and similar to the prophetic oracles. In their prophetic capacity they address Christians and churches of all time. The letters are not independent and separate from the book, but were written as part of the book and were not to be sent by mail. They are simple letters, almost outlines, yet grand. All have the same structure or form:

a) address and name of the church

b) prophetic messenger formula, with the title designations given to Christ in the opening vision (Rv 1:12-20)

c) "I know..." followed by an examination of conscience, in light of the values set forth in the gospel, about the situation and conduct at each church.

This resulted in either praise or condemnation. (Laodicea's situation was all negative, while the conduct at Smyrna and Philadelphia was all positive.)

d) invitation to convert, in view of the coming of the Lord
e) invitation to listen and internalize the announced message: "He who hears..."
f) promise of a special gift to the victor. The gifts appear to allude to the sacraments (baptism and the Eucharist) and the Christian Liturgy: to eat from the tree of life (bread of life), white stone and new name, morning star, white vestments, name on the book of life.

The major threat to Christian faith comes from within. The internal enemies are much more dangerous than external opposing forces. The pressures on the Church by external enemies create union and strength in the communities. Internal opposition, false teachers, loss of gospel values, and rebel Christians create division within the Church and can bring about its downfall.

The letters praised the principal virtues that characterized the good members of the communities: love, service, fidelity and endurance, adherence to the teachings of authorized teachers, and the rejection of falsehood.

The oracles of the seven letters condemned the lack of zeal, love, and enthusiasm among some members of the church, which led to pragmatism and apathy. Christians could not reconcile themselves with idols or worldly values. They were called to repentance and the conversion, to reform their lives.

The letters have much value for present-day Christians in that the virtues and faults of the first Christians are the same as ours. We, too, should read in them the urgent invitation to convert.

The problems of these seven churches continued after the writing of Revelation. Ignatius of Antioch, writing shortly after the Book of Revelation, sent several letters to the churches of that area and appeared to address the same problems and concerns that the biblical author had confronted.

18.

What did the author of the Book of Revelation mean when he called Christ the Alpha and the Omega?

The *Alpha* and the *Omega* are the first and last letters of the Greek Alphabet. They are equivalent to our *a* and *z*. The expression "the Alpha and the Omega" were used as symbols of the totality of things. The author of Revelation used the phrase, "I am the Alpha and the Omega," four times (1:8; 21:6; 22:13; see 1:17-18). The phrase was used to express God's sovereignty over history. Before anything existed and after everything that exists, there was and is always God. For that reason, a good Christian should always say: "God comes first!" The prophet Isaiah used identical terms to describe God's sovereignty and power over the destiny of nations: "I am the first and the last; besides me there is no god" (Is 44:6).

In the first part of Revelation the expression "Alpha and Omega" refers to God. In the final section of the book, the expression is applied in all its meaning to Jesus Christ: "I am the Alpha and the Omega, the first and last, the beginning and the end" (Rv 22:13). All history is enclosed in God and Christ. Nothing that exists or happens can escape his plan and his control.

Who were the Nicolaitans who lived in Ephesus, Pergamum, and Thyatira (Rv 2:1-29)?

The Nicolaitans referred to repeatedly in the second chapter of Revelation were in all probability a group of Christians who searched for ways to accommodate to the social and religious life of the Roman Empire—they compromised with the Romans so they would be allowed to participate in the social functions of the empire.

The city of Ephesus, in particular, was a center of attraction for all kinds of pagan religions and distortions of the Christian life. Ephesus had a population of 300,000; it was the *lumen Asiae*, the light of Asia. Situated at a key crossing of busy highways, Ephesus was a commercial, cultural, and religious center. In addition, the city was the headquarters of the Roman proconsul. The temple of Artemis (Diana), one of the seven wonders of the Ancient World, was located in Ephesus (Acts 19:23-40). The apostle John, who died in Ephesus, was traditionally associated with the city. The splendor of the pagan rites and ceremonies could be a temptation for some Christians who had lost their initial fervor. In the eyes of the author of Revelation, the empire was so dehumanizing and cruel that no faithful Christian could accept it.

Commentators of the Book of Revelation offer various identifying labels for the Nicolaitans, basing their opinions on the cult on the prophetic warnings contained in the letters to the churches of Ephesus (2:1-7), Pergamum (2:12-17), and Thyatira (2:18-29). They all appear to reflect the same vision of Christianity and of the empire.

1) The Nicolaitans called themselves apostles but they were not. They were traveling missionaries who

moved about the region preaching the gospel, although in reality they searched only for an easy and comfortable life for themselves.

2) The Nicolaitans are associated with Balaam and with Jezebel (2:14-20). In the Old Testament this duo is associated with the acceptance of paganism and fornication. It is because of this that some assume that the group would compromise with simulated rites of worship, fornication, and some form of "free love." Similar faults were found in the primitive community of Corinth, where Paul, in his first letter to that community, spoke of their eating of food dedicated to the idols, and of the fornication that existed in the community. Paul reminds Christians that they should not let themselves be deceived by pretenses of liberty or superior knowledge. The only thing that matters and that should guide the life of a Christian is love.

3) There are some who see in the Nicolaitans gnostic Christians who embraced the Roman culture and religion. Their practices had been liberalized and secularized in such a way that they could not see the conflict between their pagan practices and the requirements of Christianity. The First Letter of Paul to the Corinthians told of Christians who ate meat sacrificed to the idols, and of Christians who arrogated to themselves special and profound knowledge (see 1 Cor 2:10; 4:8; Rv 2:24; 3:17). Knowledge should be guided and defined by love.

4) Many associate the Nicolaitans to one of the first seven deacons, Nicholas of Antioch (Acts 6:5). Their conclusions, however, have no serious basis.

What was the "synagogue of Satan" in the city of Smyrna?

The word *synagogue* signifies congregation or reunion. Jews used the term to designate their temples or houses of prayer outside of the Temple of Jerusalem. The term also applied to the people who congregated in these houses.

Many Jews took refuge and established themselves in Smyrna, the modern Izmir, after the destruction of the Temple of Jerusalem in A.D. 70. There they prospered and gradually revealed their hostility toward Christians; Christians were forbidden to call themselves Jews, associate with Jews, or call their groups synagogues. The Jews, who considered themselves far superior, slandered the poor and humble Christians before the imperial authorities and called for their persecution. The author of Revelation concluded that these Jews were doing the work of Satan and deserved to be called "synagogue of Satan."

The letter to the church of Smyrna alluded to the social and religious conditions of that city in the first century. Located north of Ephesus, Smyrna was a great commercial center with a good harbor. It had been a proud ally of Rome for nearly 300 years and had earned the title "Smyrna the Faithful." The letter reminded Christians that true glory did not come from being faithful to Rome, but from being faithful to Christ.

The letter appeared to address the problems of discouraged and spiritless Christians. This letter did not contain reproaches or denunciations, but praises. The poor had to be consoled and encouraged to look upon themselves as the "synagogue of God," the ones truly called and gathered by God to form the real Israel of the New Covenant.

What was the "throne of Satan" that was located in Pergamum (Rv 2:12-17)?

The letter to the church at Smyrna spoke of the synagogue of Satan, referring to the hostility of the Jews against Christians. In the letter to the Christians of Pergamum, their attention was drawn to the throne of Satan and the hostility of the Romans against the rising Christian Church.

Pergamum was a city famous for its religious monuments, especially its temple in honor of Aesculapius (Asklepios), god of healing. The city had been the capital of the region, center of art and culture, and maintained a library with more than 200,000 volumes. According to the Roman writer, Pliny, "pergama paper," the oldest known parchment, made of the skins of animals, was invented there and was produced in mass quantities and was instrumental in the propagation of culture.

Pergamum distinguished itself for its zeal in worshipping the emperor. It was the first city in Asia to build a temple for Emperor Augustus (29 B.C.). The phrase, "throne of Satan," may have referred to the residence of the Roman governor proconsul of the city who promoted the imperial cult and the splendid buildings that housed their pagan religion.

The author of Revelation understood the problems facing Christians. They had to remain intolerant of the cultural and religious system of the empire—a system that deified the emperor and the city of Rome; Christ and Satan had nothing in common. Antipas had remained loyal to his faith, and for his fidelity to Jesus, he was executed (Rv 2:13). The Nicolaitans (Rv 2:14) advocated ceremonial arrangements and false compromises with a social and religious syncretism. The faithful Christian was not to eat idolatrous food, but the "manna" of Christ (Rv 2:17); his title and name in glory was not to be "citizen of Rome," but "Christian" (22:4; 2:17).

22.

Who was Jezebel who lived in Thyatira (Rv 2:18-28)?

The city of Thyatira was not as important as its neighbor Pergamum. There was, however, a Roman garrison there that was responsible for the security and protection of all roads in the area. Thyatira had small textile industries, cloth-dying, leather, ceramics, and copper (see Acts 16:14-15). The industrial work force was organized around guilds or labor associations. Christians who belonged to these guilds had problems of conscience in that they were expected to participate in the political and religious functions of the guilds as dictated by the imperial cult. In this kind of situation there was always the danger of adopting syncretistic thinking and accepting the cults and their customs.

In the Old Testament, Jezebel was the wife of the king of Israel, Ahab. Through her influence, she introduced Israel to idolatry and seduced the king. She was the personal enemy of the prophet Elijah whom she sought to kill. In the Bible, the name Jezebel is used as the symbol and embodiment of evil and of the idolatrous woman who leads to sin.

John, in talking about Jezebel in the Book of Revelation, appears to be referring to a woman with a self-claimed prophetic charisma who taught a mysterious and secret doctrine on the "profundities of Satan" (vs. the "profundities of God" which is referred to in 1 Cor 2:10 and 4:8). Like the Nicolaitans, Jezebel favored adapting the Christian religion to pagan cults. This perversion of true prophecy was "fornication" in the biblical language of the Old Testament. Jezebel succeeded in presenting herself as a Christian emulator of the sibyl (Sambethe) who kept a sanctuary in Thyatira.

At the beginning of the letter to Thyatira we find the expression "Son of God" (Rv 2:18). It is the only time this expression appears in Revelation. At the end of the letter, God's function as King and Judge is underscored. It was necessary to awaken Christians to resist the false prophetess who preached a Christian laxity to adapt and accept the sun god-king that was popular in Thyatira. Christians had to keep in mind that the only sun and king was Jesus.

23.

How can one be alive and dead at the same time, as was said of the church in Sardis (Rv 3:1-6)?

The church in Sardis was in a state of spiritual coma, a lethargic mortal sleep. The inhabitants of Sardis were famous for their comfort-loving lust. The people of Sardis especially adored Cybele, the goddess of nature, and celebrated great orgies to make their fields and animals fertile and reproductive.

Sardis had been the capital of Lydia at a time when its king, Croesus, enjoyed universal fame for the city's wealth and luxurious living. The city had an almost impregnable defensive stronghold, the acropolis, but twice it had fallen into the hands of its enemies due to neglect and lack of vigilance (see Rv 3:3). The city also had a flourishing wool industry that made beautiful white garments (see Rv 3:4).

The Christian community of Sardis, surrounded by paganism, succumbed to the temptation of self-satisfaction. John denounced the community because, although legally it could have been impeccable, pastorally it was almost dead. They were Christians in appearance only.

The sin of Sardis appears to have been the bureaucratization that made everything appear normal and well on the outside, but actually left much to be desired. There was good organization but little spirit. The few Christians who had remained faithful and alert had the obligation and mission to awaken and open the eyes of the rest. Together they

50

could take the initiative and produce a spiritual flowering that would carry the Christian message to the surrounding world.

The allusion to the book of life, or the book of the living (Rv 3:5) assumes, like in Exodus 32:32, that a book existed with the names of all people living on earth. With the development of the doctrine of the Resurrection, however, there emerged the idea of a book listing those who will live in heaven (see Dan 12:1).

24.

Why does the church in Philadelphia receive special treatment (Rv 3:7-13)?

Philadelphia, literally "the city of brotherly love," was a small, thriving commercial center. Like many of the surrounding communities, it had been devastated several times by earth-quakes and had been reconstructed with the help of the Roman emperor—for whom a center of worship had been established.

The letter to the church in Philadelphia is the most personal and encouraging of all seven letters. It speaks insistently—seven times—in the first person. Philadelphia receives generous praises filled with tenderness, and is neither attacked nor criticized. It was a church that had struggled to remain faithful, and would struggle even more in the future. John was gentler with this community than with the others, perhaps because the Philadelphia community was small and humble; the few Christians there, who felt weak and powerless, were encouraged to continue to resist intimidation and the attacks of the Jews. They had persevered with patience during trying times, and now the messenger exhorts them to endure the last trial and final test.

John announced that the Jews who were persecuting them would one day come to realize that Christians are the true Israel of God. God would reward their fidelity by opening

51

wide the door of conversions, while closing all doors to persecutors. A Christian victory was assured.

The victors were told that they would become pillars in the Temple of God; they would receive pubic glory similar to the glory of the victorious Roman generals who had their names written on columns located within their temples. The names of the Christian victors would forever be memorials in the Temple of God. The author appears to suggest that Christians will enjoy this familiarity with God and "will know his name" in such a way as to almost be on first-name terms with him.

25.

What is the special danger in being neither cold nor hot but lukewarm (Rv 3:14-22)?

Laodicea was a city situated about three and one-half miles from Hierapolis, the source of the city's water supply. The thermal waters, originating in hot springs around Hierapolis, arrived in Laodicea lukewarm and undrinkable. Laodicea was a proud community, having fully recovered from the earthquake of A.D. 60 by their own means, without help from the Romans. It was a city that considered itself self-sufficient and able to say: "I am rich, I have prospered, and I need nothing" (Rv 3:17).

The letter to the church of Laodicea alludes to an affluent economic and social condition that gave Laodiceans an aura of security and prosperity as they gloried in the riches of their city. Laodicea had a school of medicine and pharmacology that was famous for its eye specialists. Also, there were established agricultural and commercial enterprises, with banks and money lenders whose fame reached all the way to Rome. The textile industry also flourished in Laodicea, especially the makers of black wool rugs and carpets.

The letter contained an urgent threat for the "lukewarm"

Christians, proud and blind, who had become as mundane as the environment in their city. Insipid and without character, Laodiceans were neither against God nor against the world—they were unaware of their situation. In the English language the word *Laodicean* means indifferent or neutral, alluding to an attitude of Christians that is criticized in Revelation. Christians cannot remain neutral in the political, economic, and religious world that surrounds them. They must make a decision—they must choose Christ and the gospel to carry them through the conflict and struggle.

Laodiceans had succumbed to mediocrity and lukewarmness because of their selective beliefs and false orientation in the course of adjustment and adaptation to the world that surrounded them. John branded them "poor, blind, and naked" (Rv 3:17). The material wealth of the city should be substituted for the golden purity of faith in Jesus; the ointments of their famous eye specialists should be replaced by the everlasting light of Christ. The textile industry and makers of white garments worn by true Christians were of no use in filling the profound spiritual needs of the lost community. At the end of the letter there are tender words of care and concern to encourage Christians to seek a way out of their spiritless state.

The community of Laodicea was located nine miles northwest of Colossae, a city to which Paul had directed one of his letters. The author of Revelation, like Paul, wanted Christians to distinguish themselves, not for their accommodation to the world, but for their work to convert and transform the world.

26.

How is God described in the Book of Revelation (4:1-11)?

The fourth chapter of Revelation offers a beautiful description of God in heaven. The author does not give us pictures or photos of heaven, rather, he communicates a message by means of poetic symbols taken from prophets well known to their readers.

The description of God in heaven appears to have been inspired by the narrations of the sixth chapter of Isaiah and the first chapter of Ezekiel, in which the prophets, above all else, describe the mystery of God who rules over all creation. God is greatness, firmness, stability, security, royalty, sanctity, omnipotence, eternity, tranquility, clarity, wonder and admiration; more and better than anything else imaginable.

John also appears to have in mind the image of the imperial royal court (Roman or Persian), together with the senate and advisers that accompanied the emperor. When the emperor made his solemn entrance into Rome, it was the custom for people to shout: "You are worthy, our lord and our god...." It was precisely when the Book of Revelation was being written that the emperor Domitian ruled and, according to Roman writers of his time, liked to take on the titles that the author of Revelation declared to belong exclusively to the true God: "The holy one, glory on earth, Lord and God, Lord of the earth and Lord of the world." John's description was a protest against the imperial cult.

God does not exist in isolated splendor, like the god of the wise teachers and philosophers. God is surrounded by celestial beings, angels, the elderly, the living, the center of praise and adoration. Heaven is admiration, movement, life, and amazement in the presence of God. God is presented, according to traditional custom, surrounded by a halo of light and a marvelous rainbow that makes him invisible to mortals. Just as in the Gospel of John, God is "light and sound" and color, like a spectacle that will delight its servants for all eternity.

The throne of God is the center of the universe. It is there that history and the march of time and events are decided. Christ and Christians are at the center of history. They are the only ones that give it the complete and definitive direction that God desires.

Heaven is presented as a great concert that brings together the voices of all the works of creation—first, the four living creatures and the twenty-four elders (Rv 5:9-10); then many angels (5:11-12); and finally, the rest of creation, in heaven, on earth, in the sea, and under the earth (5:13).

27.

Why is Jesus presented in the Book of Revelation as the sacrificial Lamb, when he is gloriously enthroned in heaven (5:1-14)?

The Lamb is a biblical figure with multiple symbolisms. It was the preferred victim in the Old Testament. In the Gospel of John it is initially presented as the "Lamb of God who takes away the sin of the world" (Jn 1:29); at the end of the gospel it is the Lamb who is sacrificed and dies on the cross, at the same hour as the Passover lambs were being sacrificed in the temple. In the synoptic Gospels, Jesus is the Lamb that goes to his passion as a silent and innocent victim.

In Revelation, Jesus is above all the powerful and triumphant Lamb; the Lamb who is at once presented as the Lion of Judah and the Root of David, and who has been revealed in his passion as the Messiah who triumphed over death. The Passover lamb that has been sacrificed has seven horns and seven eyes, an indication that the plenitude of power and knowledge belong to Christ who is glorified (Mt 28:16-29).

Heaven and earth come together to sing praises for God and the Lamb (Rv 5:8-9). The perfect dignity of the Lamb is described with seven attributes, that in the Old Testament, belong to God—attributions sought after by the Roman emperors to describe their own greatness: power, wealth, wisdom, strength, honor, glory, and praise. In Revelation 5:9, the Lamb answers the key question that appears in chapter

five, verse two: "Who is worthy to open the scroll and break its seals?"

Jesus, the Lamb of the Book of Revelation, is the One who controls and directs history. The secrets of history are in his hands. He is the architect who has God's plan for the construction of the history of mankind. The Lamb who is slain, yet alive, is the key in describing God's will in history; the sacrifice of Jesus on the cross is the key to understanding history.

The sacrifice makes Christ the master of history, and the will to sacrifice himself makes Christians the masters of history. The power and might of the world can only extend to death, with no control over the life that comes after death. The Roman Empire could cause death but could not give meaning to life. The history of the Roman Empire did not make sense—it had no future. The Roman emperors, who in the beginning saw the Christians as easy victims with which to amuse a nation, soon realized that the Christians were extremely dangerous in that they did not worship the Roman system nor allow themselves to be deceived by propaganda. Christians through the centuries have been called to question critically all wordly systems.

28.

Who are the twenty-four elders in the Book of Revelation (4:4; 5:8)?

God lives at the center of his people, on earth and in heaven. The twenty-four elders (mentioned twelve times in Revelation) form a kind of senate or celestial court that surrounds the throne of God and adorns it with its presence. These elders represent God's church in all its universality, the old and the new Israel, in the same way as the four living creatures that represent all creation (Rv 4:6-11). They are an embodiment of the universality of the history of the salvation of the People of God that is present before God in perpetual praise and thanksgiving.

There are many Catholic authors who see in the twenty-four elders men who are glorified, especially the great saints, patriarchs, kings, prophets, and wise-men of the Old Testament, and the twelve apostles of the New Testament.

Others see in the elders a priestly class of the kingdom of God which corresponds to the twenty-four classes of priests of Israel (see 1 Chr 24:4,7-18). They are dressed in full-length tunics like the Jewish priests, and their priestly function is to give glory and praise to God.

There are some who believe that the elders are twenty-four special angels who are always in the presence of God; they associate them with the twelve signs of the zodiac and the principal stars of each sign. The ancients associated the angels with the stars and the stars with the angels. These elders would come to symbolize the powers that control all of creation. The biblical text does not favor identifying the ancients with angels because it considers them persons redeemed by Christ (see Rv 19:4). The twenty-four elders, like the 144,000 chosen ones, represent all the People of God of the Old and the New Testament and redeemed by Jesus.

29.

What do the four living creatures in the Book of Revelation represent (4:6)?

The image of the four living creatures resembling animals is taken from Ezekiel 4:4-14; to the prophet they represent all of creation. The lion symbolizes wild animals; the eagle, birds; the ox, domesticated animals; and the man, humankind.

Representing creation, the four animals appear as the four cardinal points, with the center at the throne of God. God dominates all the forces of life; these forces have to give glory and thanks to God. The living are like masters of ceremonies that give directions to the celestial liturgy.

There are some who want to see symbolic figures in these

four living creatures, representing all that is noble, strong, wise, and quick in creation. This abstract symbolism is clearer for us than for the readers of the first century.

Some authors view these four animals as alluding to the four stellar constellations known throughout the old world: Taurus, the ox; Leo, the lion; Aguila, the eagle; and Scorpio, which in the old days was portrayed as a human. The four constellations were thought to guide the course of history, holding its secrets. For these authors, this would signify that the secrets and the forces of history and nature are all standing at the service of God.

In the second century, Irenaeus was the first person to symbolically relate the four animals with the four evangelists, even though the text of Revelation never gave any reason for doing so. The man (angel) was associated with Matthew; the lion, with Mark who opens the gospel with the preaching of John the Baptist in the desert where lions lived; the ox, with Luke who begins his gospel alluding to the sacrifices of the Old Testament in which bulls were frequently offered; the eagle, with John, for being the most exalted gospel in form and content.

30.

What do saints do in heaven? Is it true that, according to the Book of Revelation, they will sing forever (5:6-14)?

It would be more important to ask what "saints" (Christians) do on earth. John, in addition to giving information about heaven, wanted to give us hope and fortitude to live and struggle on earth. Revelation describes heaven as a communal liturgy, sublime and joyful, with periods of silence and listening, followed by symbolic action.

For John earthly liturgy was a reflection of celestial worship. Christians on earth joyfully celebrated the memory of Christ's sacrifice. Christians of his time joyfully proclaimed the grandeur and divinity of Jesus, while at the same time protesting against the titles of glory and power that the Roman emperors attributed to themselves.

The happiness enjoyed by poor and oppressed Christians alarmed and annoyed the wealthy and powerful; the Christian liturgy was always subversive, calling for conversion and change, and giving hope and strength to resist the evil slave-masters.

The Christian liturgy recalls the liberation that Christ has obtained for us. It involves an attitude of protest against all dictatorships, from the despotic control of the Roman Empire to dictatorial rule in modern times.

The Church on earth (militant) joins with the Church in heaven (triumphant) in praising God. The universal communion of the Church and all creation is found in prayer. The goal of prayer is the transformation of the universe.

John presents the saints in heaven doing what Jesus does (see 1 Jn 1:1-2): they intercede for their brethren on earth to persevere in the struggle against evil. It is important for Christians to recall at all times that throughout their struggles and tribulations, the prayers of the saints are with them.

31.

What is the significance of the seven seals of the Book of Revelation (5:1–8:1)?

Seals were used in ancient times to identify property, to give validity to documents as "marks" of ownership or protection, and as signs of important or secret things.

The book sealed with seven seals is the exclusive property of God. It contains the great secrets of his plan for salvation. This book appears to be in the form of a folded document that is gradually unfolded to reveal its contents. The opening of the seventh seal serves as an introduction to the series of the seven trumpets, after which will come the revelation of the purpose of history and Christ's final triumph.

Some authors see a connection between this document, folded and sealed, and the documents that were used to repudiate marriage contracts, especially the marital breakups within the priesthood. They came to see in this association a symbolic presentation of the divorce that will dissolve the bond between the Lamb and faithless Jerusalem before entering into the new matrimony of the Lamb with the New Jerusalem that descends from heaven.

The uncovering or opening of the seals is not to satisfy human curiosity, but to fulfill and carry out God's plan in history. Christ and Christians are the ones who truly understand history and all its contradictions.

The seals remind Christians and all humanity that the calamities of history and nature should serve to awaken the conscience to focus on God and his plans.

The first four seals will be addressed in the next question, where we will talk about the four horses with their respective horsemen. The fifth seal presents the altar of God transformed in a celestial temple similar to the Temple of Jerusalem. In the midst of tragedies, tribulations, and struggles on earth, the saints' prayers are with all Christians; this should console them and give them the strength to remain faithful. The prayers of Christians do not come from a thirst for vengeance, but from a thirst for justice and the values of God's kingdom.

The sixth seal recalls the predictions in Mark 13:24 and Matthew 24:29. The narration is identical to the descriptions of the prophets of the coming of the Day of the Lord. The chaos of the universe should remind us that "we are nothing" and that we really have to put ourselves in God's hands.

The author mentions seven classes of people who are affected by the seventh seal; he does this to denote the universality of the power and action of the triumphant Lamb who makes all nature and all people feel powerless before him. Filled with terror, they hide in caves, but there is not any hiding place that can protect and secure an evil conscience—conversion is the only way out.

During the trials and calamities that afflict humanity, the evil ones begin to feel hopeless and afraid, while the good ones (the chosen, the true believers) live in glorious expectation; they know that God controls history. The incredulous ones are the prime victims of fear. Those who believe know and trust that everything that happens to them will be for their well-being.

32.

What is the significance of the four horses in the Book of Revelation (6:1-8)?

The four horses were very popular during the first World War (1914-1918). However, the four riders who mounted the horses should probably receive as much, if not more attention. During World War I, there were numerous Protestant denominations who thought the world was coming to an end. The four horsemen announce the eschatological predictions which are also mentioned in Matthew 24 and Mark 13. The image of the four horses is inspired in Zechariah 1:8-11 and 6:1-8; the narration of their activities closely follows the canticle of Habakkuk 3:4-15.

The first horse is white and is mounted by a triumphant and invincible rider (Rv 6:2). At this stage, this horseman is not Christ, as many think. The Passover Lamb has been sacrificed and will appear only as triumphant and invincible on a white horse in chapter 19:11. This first horseman, together with his three companions, is a bearer of calamities and wars and should not be seen as a symbol of the triumphant march of the gospel across the world, as some imagine.

The first horseman is probably an Antichrist symbol who rides victoriously until Christ comes to disarm him (Rv 19:11-21). This is why he is dressed in white, like Christ, trying to imitate him (see Rv 13:1-19). The first horseman is the wolf in sheep's clothing that for a time appeared to be invincible in his projects. The author repeatedly insists that he has power only as long as God permits: "He was given power" (see Rv 6:2,4,6,8).

In the theology of the school of John, the Antichrist and the antichristians of the last days are those who leave the Church (see 1 Jn 2:18). They are the ones who make wars and create religious divisions; they are against a united Church and the Christian community. The victory of the first horseman brings calamities to humanity: death (Rv 6:4); famine (6:6); and hell (6:8). Many see proof that this is happening through the religious conflicts and wars that afflict the Church and humanity.

There are some authors who see in the description of the horseman who "had a bow" an allusion to the armor of the Parthian cavalry. The Parthians were enemies of the Roman Empire along Rome's eastern border, and had defeated (A.D. 62) the Roman legions; possibly, the author hoped for the total defeat of the empire and the liberation of Christians.

The second horseman mounts a red horse (Rv 6:3-4), symbol of blood and fire. He represents powers hostile to God and evil forces that unleash civil wars and turn brother against brother. From A.D. 41 through A.D. 69, there had been numerous civil wars within the Roman Empire.

The third horseman rides a black horse (Rv 6:5-6). He appears to be the famine that generally follows wars. Here we see that God puts limits on evil powers (6:6); the olive oil and the wine will be saved (see 2 Kgs 6:27; 7:1). In the study of Roman history we find that a great famine occurred in the Roman Empire between A.D. 42 and A.D. 51; also, during the reign of Domitian (A.D. 92), another great famine occurred, and throughout the region vineyards had to be destroyed to allow additional wheat and barley to be planted.

The fourth horseman (Rv 6:7-8), mounted on a pale green horse, appears to represent the plague or epidemic that generally follows periods of famine and wars. Death itself rides with each of the four horsemen. This horseman also has limited powers: he can only afflict one-fourth of the earth. If God limits the powers of evil, Christians are called to do the same. If they don't eliminate evil, at least they have to work to weaken and remove its effects.

Perversion and selfishness today continue to create horsemen that ride throughout all parts of the world. As we study each historical period, we should attempt to determine which are the horses of evil and their respective colors.

33.

Who are the 144,000 who are sealed (Rv 7:4-8)? Are they special saints who follow the Lamb? Do they have a special place in heaven?

These questions are important for many people who are bothered by the teachings of the Jehovah's Witnesses who say that their group comprises the 144,000 especially elected by God. The questions assume that special outings, marches, and parades occur in heaven. Remember, however, that the author of Revelation used symbolic language and that the 144,000 who walked with the Lamb are like Adam in Paradise who "walked with God" (Gn 3:8). They walk with God/ Christ, dressed in robes, with no anxieties or half fears, in eternal peace and happiness (see Rv 7:15-17).

The number "144,000" is the total of 12 x 12 x 1,000. The number "twelve" was considered to be special because it was the number of the months in a year, the number of signs in the zodiac, and the number of tribes of the Old and New Israel. The number "144" is a perfect square, a technical and appropriate number to represent the People of God. The number "1,000" was the highest number in the Jewish system. The Greeks had the "myriad" that equaled 10,000, and symbolized something immense or innumerable. The number "million" is not mentioned in Revelation because it was invented or named for the first time in Italy during the Middle Ages, just 500 years ago.

The number "144,000" is the perfect and complete number of the immense multitude that follows Christ. Just as Israel took a census in the desert after its liberation from Egypt, the army of the Lamb is counted at the start of the New Exodus. Since it is a symbolic number it should not be taken arithmetically: it stands for a quantity that is countless and imposing. That is why each tribe has the same number; for God there is no favoritism.

Apocalyptic commentators have diverse opinions about the identity of the 144,000 elected:

1. They are "virgins" in the biblical sense of the word: the ones who did not "fornicate" by adoring false idols or falling into idolatry.
2. They are the Jews of the twelve tribes of Israel who converted to Christianity.
3. They are the martyrs who joined in the sacrifice of the Lamb and triumphed with him.
4. They are special heroic Christians who follow Christ unconditionally.
5. They are the priests, because they carry a special name that denotes belonging or consecration to God.
6. They are ascetic Christians who have maintained a spiritual and corporal virginity.
7. They are the victors of the letters to the seven churches of the Book of Revelation.
8. They are the Christians of the Roman Empire who stood firm in their faith; the first ones to be rescued.
9. They are all Christians who struggled and won—not just a group or special class of saints.

It can be said that all these classes of people, in some way, belong to the 144,000—the number includes all the People of God of all times.

In the enumeration of the twelve tribes of Israel which John related to the 144,000, Judah heads the list as the messianic tribe. The tribe of Dan is omitted, and in its place the tribe of Manasseh is named. We do not know the reason for this omission, but ever since the time of Irenaeus, many have believed that it's because at the time it was thought that the Antichrist was going to come from the tribe of Dan, the first tribe to fall into idolatry. The tribe of Dan is also given very unflattering descriptions in the Old Testament (see Jgs 18:30; Jer 8:16; Dt 33:22; Gn 49:17). The symbol of the tribe of Dan was the serpent—for this reason the tribe could be associated with the devil and the Antichrist. If the 144,000 are the ones who remained faithful to God, there was no room to include the first idolatrous tribe.

34.

Who are the angels who stood before God (Rv 8:2-6)?

In Jewish tradition and in the Old Testament, special angels are frequently mentioned; angels who are almost an embodiment of God or like manifestations of his acts. At times it is difficult to distinguish if the person who is talking is God himself or an angel, as in chapters 18 and 22 of Genesis.

The Old Testament frequently mentions special angels whose mission is to instruct and guide the elected People through difficult times and to defend the elect in their struggles (see Ex 23:20-23—the mission of the guardian angel of Israel; 2 Kgs 19:35—the angel of the Lord destroys the Assyrian army of Sennacherib). These angels have special missions of salvation, and they intercede with God on behalf of the elected People.

Biblical sources also mention the seven special angels who stood before God as a parallel to certain dignitaries who had access to the throne of kings (see Tb 12:14 and Rv 8:2,6).

Jewish apocryphal books give the names of these angels—
they all end in *el*. *El* was an ancient name given to God by
the Jews; hence the special relationship with the acts of God.
The names and their meanings are as follows:

- **Raphael**—Healing or God's medicine.
- **Michael**—"Who can compare with God?"
- **Gabriel**—Strength or fortitude of God.
- **Uriel**—Fire of God.
- **Raguel**—Friend of God.
- **Sariel**—Prince of God.
- **Remiel**—Height of God.

Revelation, following Jewish belief, frequently alludes to
special angels of high rank. Many see these angels as poetic
figures who help describe acts of God. In Revelation 1:4 and
5:6, we find reference to the seven spirits who stand before
God; Revelation 4:5 speaks of seven flaming torches that
appear to refer to these angels.

35.

What is the meaning of the seven trumpets of the Book of Revelation (8:6–9:21)? How do they relate to the seven seals?

In biblical times, the trumpet was an instrument that could
be heard from very long distances. More than an instrument
of music, it was used as a sign of alarm and to gather the
people. The trumpet announced the festivities and victories
of the communities: it was also used to direct combatants
engaged in battle. Eventually, however, the trumpet became
a traditional eschatological instrument. Paul mentioned the
trumpet in relation to the resurrection of the dead and the
Final Judgment.

The trumpets of the Book of Revelation were urgent and

alarming calls to conversion because the end is near. The plagues heralded by the trumpets were described in terms of the plagues of Egypt (Ex 7-10). The objects mentioned in relation to the trumpets remind us today of some of the objects used in the liturgy of the Temple of Jerusalem: trumpets, wine glasses, coals, perfumes, and the altar. All of nature is like a great Temple of God.

The plagues announced by the trumpets allude to natural phenomena and historical events of the author's era. He described them in an epic and poetic style in order to stir emotions and feelings that lead to conversion.

Natural phenomena and catastrophes of history should be seen as signs of human limitations; likewise, Jesus looked upon rain not only as a natural phenomenon but as a divine gift from the Father for the just and the unjust (see Mt 5:45). The events of nature are urgent calls to conversion because the end is drawing closer.

The presentation of the trumpets is arranged, like the seven seals, in series of four, then three. The first four trumpets, like the first four seals, are a unified group; they do not directly affect the people but do affect the places where they live and work. Nature becomes unhinged and violent—like in the days of the plagues of Egypt and of Sodom and Gomorrah.

The author again reminds us that in the case of the trumpets, like in the seven seals, the events of heaven and earth are intimately related, and we should live the history of the earth in communion with heaven.

The plagues of the first four trumpets are not total; only one-third of the earth suffers its consequences, and there is still time and space for conversion. The effects of each plague affect three things:

- 1st trumpet — One third of the earth turns to fire, affecting earth, trees, and green plants.
- 2nd trumpet — One third of the sea turns to blood, affecting water, marine life, ships.

- 3rd trumpet — One third of all potable water turns to poison, affecting rivers, springs, waterways.
- 4th trumpet — One third of all light turns to darkness, affecting the sun, moon, stars.

The first plagues have affected things more than people. The fifth and sixth plagues are described in terrifying terms, with armies in hellish appearance that make war against people, but do not achieve the desired results. Although God moves the powers of heaven, earth, and even hell to call the wicked to conversion, the human heart can still resist until the end. All the power of God cannot change the willful hardness of the hearts of people.

The last two plagues allude to the Parthian invasions that came from the east, which had defeated the Romans and conquered Jerusalem 100 years before. The defeat of the Roman legions had not been forgotten, nor avenged; the Parthians were an irresistible enemy that was at the doors of the empire, and the author thought they would bring its destruction.

The Parthians were like locusts (multitude); they rode horses (speed) and easily surrounded the slow and heavily-loaded Roman legions. They were like lions (ferocious) in battle; like birds they reached everywhere (no one could avoid them); they were men (intelligent beings) who knew well the enemy's tricks. The Parthian cavalry was universally known and feared.

Every war and every invasion is a presage of the end. We must learn from history and live in readiness. Penance, as the Bible repeatedly teaches, can change the course of history.

Is it true that the poisonous star has fallen from the sky and is now destroying the earth (Rv 8:10)?

No, but many preachers have been saying that it has, some by alluding to the acid rain that is destroying forests and meadows, others in referring to the nuclear catastrophe at Chernobyl in the Soviet Union. Revelation says: "The third angel blew his trumpet, and a great star fell from heaven, blazing like a torch, and it fell on a third of the rivers and on the springs of water. The name of the star is Wormwood. A third of the waters became wormwood, and many died from the water, because it was made bitter" (Rv 8:10:11).

It is a coincidence that the word *chernobyl*, the name of the place in Russia where the tremendous radioactive leak occurred, means "wormwood." The damages from the escape of radioactive material have been extensive throughout Russia and other regions of Europe.

Fundamentalist preachers who are always looking for things that justify their fantasies and interpretations have seized upon these events in Russia. They are the ones who, after the explosion of an atomic bomb, sat back and waited for the "prediction" of the Book of Revelation to come true. These same preachers also have related the acid rain of recent years to the rain of blood mentioned in Revelation 8:7.

In his style of writing, the biblical author alluded to events of his time. He described happenings in epic style, at times exaggerated, as part of a narrative and educational process. The wormwood (see Jer 23:15; 9:15; Am 6:12) was used to poison water so enemies could not drink from them. In this case God, in a new but traditional design, fights with his enemies as a way of calling them to conversion.

Will armies of monsters appear on earth at the end of the world, as chapter nine of the Book of Revelation says?

The fifth and sixth trumpets of Revelation, according to the text, announce that God brings into play the powers of heaven and hell in order to call the wicked to conversion. Some fundamentalists like to give free rein to their imagination, and they reach extremes of exaggeration more than the apocalyptic authors themselves. There are some, for example, who associate the "monsters" of Revelation with soldiers wearing gas masks that enable them to breathe the "infernal smoke" of war.

From a theological viewpoint, it could be said that the only truly monstrous element is the hardened human heart that crushes its own fellow creatures and resists God. In the fifth and sixth trumpets, hell attacks only the wicked because hell has no power over the faithful. The test makes the faithful better and the wicked worse. The plagues have been and always will be directed at the oppressors of the City of God: Egypt, Babylon, and the Roman Empire.

The description of the last two trumpets is based on texts of the Old Testament, and on the political and military conditions of the time of the author. The first five plagues announced by the trumpets are based on Exodus, with minor modifications taken from the Book of Wisdom. The fifth and sixth trumpets echo the description of the second plague of Egypt found in the Book of Wisdom: *"You sent upon them a multitude of irrational creatures to punish them, / so that they might learn that one is punished by the very things by which one sins. / For your all-powerful hand, / which created the world out of formless matter, / did not lack the means to send upon them a multitude of bears, or bold lions, / or newly-created unknown beasts full of rage, / or*

71

*such that breathe out of fiery breath, / or belch forth a thick
pall of smoke, / or flash terrible sparks from their eyes; / not
only could the harm they did destroy people, / but the mere
sight of them could kill by fright. / Even apart from these,
people could fall at a single breath / when pursued by justice
/ and scattered by the breath of your power. / But you have
arranged all things by measure and number and weight"* (Wis
11:15-20; see Joel 2:4-11).

The author of Revelation, besides being inspired in the
Old Testament, appears to keep in mind the Parthian armies
operating in the area of the Euphrates River who threatened
the stability of the Roman Empire. Several invasions of Pal-
estine had come from the Euphrates (Babylon), a proverbial
symbol of the hostility toward God. The Parthians were a
fantastic and irresistible enemy; their swift cavalry and their
ferociousness in battle would come to level everything in their
path. The end of the empire was at hand.

38.

What is the meaning of the mysterious
small scroll in the Book of Revelation
(10:1-11)?

In chapters ten and eleven of Revelation, we find two
visions through which the author presents his prophetic mission of denouncing the wicked and encouraging the faithful.
The first one is similar to Ezekiel 3:1-3, where the order is
given to eat the small scroll; the second is like the version of
Zechariah 2:5-9, with the command to measure the Temple
of Jerusalem.

Before the prophet can preach God's word, he must eat
and digest the scroll. The book that contains the gospel of
Jesus is an open book—it contains no secrets, and its message is for everyone. The message is bittersweet. To be called
by God is a great honor and source of pleasure, but it may
also fill the prophet with much bitterness, as the "confes-

sions" of prophet Jeremiah testify (see Jer 20:7-18; 11:21; 15:10-21).

For Christians, evangelizing and prophesying may seem to be sweet and romantic adventures; in the long run, however, if they are taken seriously, they will bring periods of intense bitterness and tribulation, which is what Jesus told his disciples to expect. The world will refuse to listen and to believe and will end by turning against the messengers. Christianity offers a broad dimension of hope and consolation for all Christians, but contains a capacity to denounce as well; the latter should serve to jolt those who live for their selfish interests.

39.

Why was John commanded to measure the Temple of God in Jerusalem (Rv 11:1-2)?

The order to measure the Temple of Jerusalem, from a historical viewpoint, is quite strange and seems out of place because the Temple had already been destroyed by the Romans at the time that John was writing his book.

To take measurements of the Temple is a sign of the divine protection that a holy place enjoys. Ezekiel meticulously measured the holy place in preparation for the coming of the glory of God, the sanctified and protective presence of God in his city (see Ez 40-43). Zechariah measured the city of Jerusalem as a prelude to the announcement of the divine protection of the city (see Zec 2:5-9).

In Revelation, John did not refer to the material or physical Temple of Jerusalem, but to the Christian community that will be protected throughout all tribulations. The community is the new Temple of God (see 1 Cor 3:16; 2 Cor 6:16; Eph 2:19-21; 1 Pt 2:5).

Just like ancient Israel suffered the tribulation of King Antiochus Epiphanes for three and one-half years, the

Church—the new Israel—will experience a short period of persecution. The forces of evil will not emerge victorious, however, because Christians are protected by God and his shepherds who sacrifice themselves for them.

40.

Who are the two witnesses in the Book of Revelation (11:3-14)?

This question is frequently raised when examining the writings of Revelation. Answers vary considerably, probably because the author refers to two historical figures whom he describes with the characteristics of several biblical figures. The principal opinions are as follows:

a) Some commentators note that the description of the two witnesses brings Moses to mind (water turned into blood), and Elijah (fire from heaven) whose appearances, in the Jewish tradition, were expected at the end of the world (see Dt 18:15; Mal 3:22-24).

b) Others see in this narration allusion to chapter four of Zechariah who mentions a lamp stand of gold with two olive trees—Zerubbabel and Joshua the priest, the two "anointed" of the community. These two witnesses would represent the priestly and regal mission of the Church.

c) There are those who consider the witnesses to be two Christians who lived in the first century and died as martyrs for their beliefs. The author uses these well-known figures as models for his readers.

d) It has been popular to identify the two witnesses with Elijah and Enoch—two very important figures in the Old Testament who were spared death because of their righteousness. These two would come at the end of time to give testimony of the Messiah and to face death with the rest of humanity.

e) Some see the apostles Peter and Paul as the two witnesses. The preaching of the two apostles had resounded throughout the empire, and they had shared the death and the triumph of Christ.

f) Other authors conclude that the two witnesses are two symbolic figures who represent and embody the prophets of the Church. The witnesses are two because, according to ancient law, two was the required number to corroborate a testimony. Pagan society cannot get rid of the prophets nor erase them from their thoughts because the blood of martyrs is the seed of Christians. Some prophets die, but others arise, encouraged by the same Spirit, to carry out their mission.

The ancient prophets had been seen as a plague that brought annoyance and uneasiness to the kings and to the wealthy and powerful leaders of Israel. The Church and the Christians were the plague for the idolatrous empire that considered itself lord of the universe. Christians should not fear the struggle, however, because their true and total triumph will be through their death, as it was through the death of Christ.

41.

Who is the woman in chapter twelve of the Book of Revelation?

The vision of the woman and the dragon contains many details which commentators use to present their personal interpretations of this apocalyptic event.

Catholic authors generally see three possibilities for interpretation: identifying the woman with the Synagogue

(Judaism), the Church (the Christian community), and the Blessed Virgin Mary. The last possibility will be addressed in the next question.

In the biblical symbolism of the Old Testament that appears in Revelation, a woman generally represents a community, a city, or a nation. The "daughter of Zion" is Jerusalem, the woman Samaritan who met Jesus at the well is the city of Samaria, and the whore who sits on the beast is the city of Rome with its empire.

The woman of Revelation is presented as mother of the Messiah who rules all nations with an iron rod. It is said that she has other children and that the dragon continues to fight against them (Rv 12:17). The glorious woman from heaven becomes a poor woman who is persecuted on earth; she is taken to the desert where she has a safe place prepared by God. These last two apocalyptic images point to the Church or Christian community.

The Church, beginning with Calvary, is what gives birth to Christ in history; it also gives birth to Christians. All efforts of the dragon—the Roman Empire—against the Church are condemned to fail. The community of ancient Israel was taken by God to the desert on eagle wings (see Ex 19:4) to protect her from the Egyptian dragon, and the community of the New Covenant will likewise be protected by God. The woman's labor pains remind us of the eschatological prophecies of salvation that the prophets promised Israel (see Is 54:1-6; 49:21; Mi 4:9-10; Is 26:16-19). Those prophecies are fulfilled with the birth of the new Jerusalem, the Church.

The vision of the woman announces the birth of a new humanity in the Church. In the old humanity of Adam and Eve, the dragon (the serpent) was lying in wait and won a short-lived victory, but in the new humanity, sin has no present and no future.

Some authors note reflections of a transcultural myth in the narration of the woman because the old legends of Babylon and Egypt also talked about a goddess who was about to give birth and a dragon who threatened to carry off the child when the child was born. However, it was carried off to safety in heaven. The author here is not thinking of pagan symbolism, but of the birth of a new humanity which parallels the birth of humanity beginning with Adam and Eve.

42.

Is it true that the woman in chapter twelve of the Book of Revelation is the Virgin of Guadalupe?

Protestant commentators, with few exceptions, see in the woman of Revelation a representation of the People of God from the Old and New Testaments. A few Catholic commentators somehow relate the woman to Mary, the Virgin of Nazareth, for being the mother of him who crushed the head of the serpent (see Gn 3:15). This would mean that Mary, more than being the woman of Revelation, would be the New Eve and the mother of believers.

Many Catholic commentators relate the woman to Mary in three different ways:

1. The author talks of the Church with descriptions resembling Mary.
2. The text talks of Mary inasmuch as she is an archetype of the Church.
3. Mary and the Church occupy the author's thoughts at the same time.

We should note that apocalyptic symbols are ambivalent: they may refer directly to the People of God in the Old and New Testaments, to a celestial Jerusalem, and indirectly to the Mother of Jesus. The vision of Revelation describes the mystery of Calvary, a mystery that was presented theologically in the fourth gospel. There, Jesus goes to glory, Mary becomes mother again, and the Church is born.

The Fathers of the Church of the first eight centuries saw the Church in the woman of Revelation, including the Old and New Testaments. Writers of recent times began associating the woman with Mary, especially in proposing the doctrine of the Assumption of Mary. The liturgy of the feast of the Assumption, from 1950, contains direct allusions to the text of Revelation.

In the eighteenth century, it became popular in Mexico to identify the woman of Revelation with Our Lady of Guadalupe. Today, Guadalupe mariologists insist on that identification and attempt to justify the association with their own interpretation of the biblical text. It could be said, however, that even if the biblical text did not look to the future—to Guadalupe—Our Lady could nonetheless look clearly into the past, to the text of the Bible.

The French mariologist René Laurentin talks about how God and the Virgin make their appearances in the form and style of communication appropriate to where each vision takes place. They make use of signs that allow them to be recognized according to the message to be communicated. To Laurentin, the light of the sun that robes Our Lady of Guadalupe suggests the woman of Revelation, clothed with the sun, with a crown of twelve stars, who comes to earth to take part in a painful new birth in our world.

Father Virgilio Elizondo, an expert on Guadalupe and a well-known theologian throughout the United States, has associated the appearance of Our Lady with the pictorial language of the Aztecs. Indeed, the image of the Virgin was a lesson in theology: the Virgin was superior to the Aztec sun god in that she could eclipse the sun with her body. In addition, she was superior to the moon goddess under her feet. She was important because an angel carried her in his arms, and with her brown face, head bowed, and the palms of her hands pressed together, she was not a goddess but a human being. She dressed like a woman with child, indicating she was about to give birth.

Father Elizondo also sees in Our Lady of Guadalupe the woman of Revelation who appears to a suffering and conquered nation to give birth to a new people, the mestizo and Christian people of Mexico. A new personality and identity for Latin America is born with Our Lady of Guadalupe. There, a glorious and triumphant mother brings a new birth of faith and hope to her oppressed children.

43.

Who is the dragon of the Book of Revelation?

The dragon in chapter twelve of Revelation is described as "the ancient serpent, who is called the devil and Satan, the deceiver of the whole world" (12:9). The author was convinced that the devil mobilized the power and might of the Roman Empire against the Christian community.

The figure of the dragon brings to mind two recorded events in the beginning of creation. The first is the fall of the angels who rebelled against God (see Rv 13:4 "Who can compare with God?"); the second is the temptation of Adam and Eve. Today, like them, the dragon is waiting, ready to destroy God's plan. The New Eve, however, the woman of Revelation, emerges victorious with God's help.

The dragon has seven heads with seven diadems. The tail of the red dragon sweeps away a third of the stars in the sky and hurls them down to the earth. The dragon is a poor imitation of the Lamb, who is the true King, all-powerful, and controlling the course of history (see Rv 1:16-18; 5:6; 19:12). The devil wants to imitate God and works to establish the anti-kingdom of God in the world.

The dragon symbolizes the basic impotence of the forces of evil who challenge the People of God. The dragon is impotent in heaven and on earth. He fails in his intent to devour the child about to be born and is unsuccessful in his persecution of the woman because the earth swallows the torrent of water he spews out after her. He will not be successful in his persecution of the Christian community, either. But the devil will continue being a threat because he is desperate.

The text repeats three times "the dragon was thrown down to earth" (Rv 12:9). The defeat of Satan is caused by the triumph and exaltation of Jesus on Calvary when the child was taken up to God and his throne. When Jesus was exalted, the devil lost his ascendancy over mankind: "Now is the judgment of this world; now the ruler of this world will be driven out. And I, when I am lifted up from the earth, will draw all people to myself. Jesus said this to indicate the kind of death he would die" (Jn 12:31-33).

44.

What do the beasts in chapter thirteen of the Book of Revelation represent?

The two beasts in chapter thirteen of Revelation, together with the dragon, form a satanical trinity that parodies the Trinity of God. The first beast is the Antichrist who attempts to create an anti-kingdom; the second beast is the prophet of the Antichrist who works to insure his triumph.

The activity of the two beasts who pursue the elected of God explains how the dragon continues its war against the woman's children (Rv 12:1-17). The dragon has given its own power to the beasts just as Jesus transmitted his power and mission to his disciples.

The first beast is an embodiment of the dragon's powers. Both monsters have seven heads, ten horns, and ten diadems. The description of the beast contains elements of the four beasts described in Daniel (7:4-6). They all refer to a political reality, a symbol of the persecutors of Christians—the Roman Empire and its successors—who are the political and economic powers who wage war against the kingdom of God. The narration of Revelation alludes directly and in detail to the extent of Roman might and the arrogance of the emperor who laid claim to divine titles: "The beast was given a mouth uttering haughty and blasphemous words, and it was allowed to exercise authority for forty-two months. It opened its mouth to utter blasphemies against God, blaspheming his name and his dwelling, that is, those who dwell in heaven. Also it was allowed to make war on the saints and to conquer them. It was given authority over every tribe and people and language and nation, and all the inhabitants of the earth will worship it, everyone whose name has not been written from the foundation of the world in the Book of Life of the Lamb that was slaughtered" (Rv 13:5-8).

One of the beast's heads seemed to have been mortally wounded, but this mortal wound was healed; this is an echo of the resurrection of Jesus (Rv 13:3). The beast, the power of evil, is always present in history; it recovers from its mortal wounds and always finds a way to regenerate itself. Christians throughout history cannot defeat evil "once and for all." They will have to do battle in each generation to keep evil forces from lifting their heads to do harm. There will be times, however, when a Christian physically will not be able to escape the pressing evil powers; the Christian must then be prepared to die for his convictions: *If you are to be taken captive, / into captivity you go; / if you kill with the sword, / with the sword you must be killed./Here is a call for the endurance and faith of the saints"* (Rv 13:10).

Many commentators see in the beast who recovers from his wounds the Roman Emperor, Nero, who was the first persecutor of Christians, and who was assassinated. Nero was so cruel and eccentric that Christians and pagans feared him even after his death. Roman historians cite evidence that many people could not believe he was really dead—*Nero redivivus*—and feared he would return to rule Rome. When, thirty years after Nero, the Emperor Domitian began his persecution of Christians, many believed that it was really Nero who had come back to life.

The second beast is the prophet of the Antichrist, a false

prophet who also serves the first beast. The author of Revelation alluded to the oppressive powers of the Romans and how they made social life impossible for Christians who lived in Asia Minor and throughout the region of the seven churches of the Book of Revelation.

The first beast mimics Christ in glory. The second beast, in the figure of a Lamb, but with two horns and no diadems, appears to mimic the acts of the Holy Spirit. Just as the Holy Spirit performed miracles in the early Church, the second beast attempted to deceive people with his own signs and wonders.

The description of the actions of the second beast brings to mind the false prophet, Simon the Magician, who used his magical art to make people believe he embodied the power and authority of God (see Acts 8:9-17). A Roman governor in Asia Minor had taken drastic measures to force all the people to worship the emperor (see Rv 13:16-17). From Roman historians we learn that something similar occurred some years later, during the time of the Emperor Trajan. Pagan priests did not have any scruples about using ventriloquism and trickery to deceive the people.

In social, political, and religious life, everyone is sealed, stamped, or marked; some are identified with the seal of God, others are stamped with the mark of the beast (see Rv 13:16-18 and 14:1). The fruits of their struggles and efforts reveal the seal they carry.

45.

What does the number "666," the number of the beast, represent?

When speaking about the symbolism of numbers, we said that number "six" denotes imperfection because it is less than the number "seven" that signifies perfection. When the number is repeated three times it represents imperfection in the superlative form.

The number "666" is introduced in a verse that invites the reader to reflect on the implication of the passage: "This calls for wisdom: let anyone with understanding calculate the number of the beast, for it is the number of a person. Its number is six hundred sixty-six" (Rv 13:18). The author wanted readers to understand that he writes about something occurring among them.

Before the system of Arabic numerals was invented, Jews, Greeks, and Romans used the letters of the alphabet as numbers. As a result, every name or word had a numerical value equal to the sum of its letters. The author of Revelation was thinking of the name or title of the beast, well known to Christians, whose sum of the letters equals 666.

In all probability, the author was thinking of the name or title of Emperor Nero, who was beastly and cruel. In fact, the Hebrew letters of the words "Nero Caesar" add up to 666:

<u>N</u>	<u>R</u>	<u>W</u>	<u>N</u>		<u>Q</u>	<u>S</u>	<u>R</u>		
50	200	6	50		100	60	200	=	666

There are many who don't believe in Nero as a suitable candidate for the beast since he had died twenty-five years earlier. But, as we said in the discussion of the last question, the author was referring directly to Emperor Domitian, who often claimed blasphemous titles such as "Caesar-god" that added up to 666. This ruthless dictator and persecutor of Christians indeed was establishing himself as a new Nero.

Throughout the course of history, people have attempted to assign the number of the beast to different world leaders and personalities: The pope, Martin Luther, Joseph Stalin, Adolf Hitler, Fidel Castro, and others. The ruling beast symbolizes and embodies the might and power of evil that wants to conquer the faithful and destroy the Christian community. It is important, therefore, to practice prudence and charity when judging others.

46

What is the mark or seal stamped on the condemned in the Book of Revelation (14:9-11;16:16)?

The mark of the beast corresponds to the seal of the Lamb discussed in Revelation 7:2-4. All of mankind is marked in some way by Christ-God, or by the devil. Before the crucified Christ and before the sacrificed Lamb, no one can remain neutral. According to their individual acts of faith, some will rise to the kingdom of God, and others will fall into the realm of the Antichrist.

When speaking of the mark or sign of the beast, the author of Revelation was looking to the Old Testament and the plight of Christians who lived in the area of the seven churches and who were under the jurisdiction of the Roman Empire. The seal or mark was used to identify persons, property, and possessions; the stamp could also express dignity and status. Cain was the first person to be sealed by God. He was marked by the Lord, lest anyone should try to kill him (see Gn 4:15). In Exodus, Jewish homes were marked with the blood of the Passover lamb to protect them against the final plague that destroyed their first-born (12:7-13). In Ezekiel, all persons marked with the seal of God were saved from death (9:4,6).

All those marked with the blood or name of the Lamb will be protected and will reign in the celestial Jerusalem (Rv 7:2-4; 14:1; 22:4). Christians are sealed at baptism with the blood of Christ, and like Jesus, they are also sealed with the Holy Spirit. They have nothing to fear.

The sign of protection and dignity for Christians is the letter *T* representing the sign of the cross. Some see in this *T* the Hebrew word *TMM* (Temam), meaning innocent. According to some beliefs, the sign of the beast is the letter *alef*, which refers to the word '*RR* (Arur) meaning cursed (see Dt 27-28).

The author of Revelation was also thinking of the situation of the Christians in Asia Minor who had been declared undocumented and illegal by the Roman authorities. By order of the Roman governor of the region, all persons who participated in the sacrifices of the imperial cult received a document or certificate authorizing them to buy and sell goods and services and to obtain employment to earn a living. Christians who lacked this official document encountered many hardships and found it almost impossible to lead any kind of social life. But those who accepted the stamp of that "beast" and abandoned their faith were destined to be condemned. They saved their physical life but lost eternal life.

47.

What is the song of Moses and of the Lamb in chapter fifteen of the Book of Revelation?

The author of Revelation continually refers to the Book of Exodus, especially to chapter fifteen, which describes the plagues of Egypt and the sanctuary or tent of testimony that was a sign of the protective presence of God before his People.

The author reiterates throughout his narratives the theme of hope and faith for all Christians; as fear and uncertainty continue to grow and pervade the earth, Christians must pause, reflect, and look to heaven. This will bring fresh promise and encouragement to remain faithful, while offering a clear view of the punishment that awaits the wicked and evil around them. It is because of this look at heaven that the vision of the seven bowls is interrupted; previously, the cycle of the seven trumpets had been interrupted with a view of celestial liturgy (Rv 8:1-5).

Before the final punishment of Babylon/Rome, God will once again send plagues similar to the disaster cast upon

Egypt. Unfortunately, the wicked will harden their hearts, just like the Egyptian pharaoh.

The true exodus is not the one that occurred in Egypt nor after the fall of Babylon. It is that of Christ and of Christians who are liberated from the power of death and the agents of Satan (Lk 9:31). The Christians wanted to be liberated from the oppressive empire that either sentanced them to death or tried to enslave them.

John saw the elect standing together on a sea of glass mingled with fire; the victorious elect were singing a song of Moses and of the Lamb, imitating the People of Israel after crossing the Red Sea. The song of the Book of Revelation is quite different from the song of Exodus. It bears a relationship to the text of the Book of Deuteronomy. Like the song of the Old Testament, the song of Moses praises the greatness of God, the works of God, and God's justice, truth, and judgment. The song of Moses and the song of the Lamb are one: the hymn of the totality of the chosen People of the Old and New Testaments who are liberated by God.

48.

What is the meaning of the seven bowls of the Book of Revelation (15:5; 16:21)? How do they relate to the seven trumpets and to the seven seals?

The seven bowls in chapter fifteen of Revelation explain events announced in Revelation 14:6-12. God continues his punishment of the wicked in order to call them to conversion. The seven angels hold in their hands bowls or chalices similar to the cups used in the liturgy of the Temple of Jerusalem. The plagues of the bowls are not limited in quantity or space, and they affect the entire universe. Their purpose is to remove all obstacles to the establishment of the kingdom of God. These plagues are similar to the plagues of the seven trumpets, and are an eschatological interpretation of the

plagues of Egypt described in Exodus 7-10. In Revelation we find the following:

SEALS	TRUMPETS	BOWLS
6:1-8:6	8:7-12; 9:1-19; 11:15-19	16:1-12,17-21
1. White horse: bloody wars 6:1-2	**1. Upon the earth:** hail and fire mixed with blood 8:7	**1. Upon the earth:** boils and sores 16:2
2. Red horse: civil war 6:3-4	**2. Into the sea:** burning mountain sea of blood 8:8-9	**2. Over the sea:** turns to blood 16:3
3. Black horse: famine 6:5-6	**3. Falling star:** bitter waters 8:10-11	**3. Rivers, fountains, and drinking water:** turned to blood 16:4-7
4. Pale green horse: pestilence 6:7-8	**4. Over the sun:** its light fades 8:12	**4. Over the sun:** people burned by scorching heat 16:8-9
5. Prayers of martyrs: judgment of God 6:9-11	**5. Infernal locusts:** torture of people 9:1-11	**5. Over the throne of the beast:** darkness and suffering 16:10-11

SEALS	TRUMPETS	BOWLS
6. Earthquake: sun, moon and stars; destruction of earth and terror in people 6:12-17	6. Cavalry from hell: kills one-third of humanity 9:13-19	6. Over Euphrates river: dries to give passage to invaders 16:12
7. Silence: earthquake, thunder, lightning 8:1-6	7. Announcement from kingdom of God: storm, earthquake, and hail 11:15-19	7. In the air: storm, earthquake, and hail 16:17-21

The first four plagues affect the principal elements of creation and the natural world: land, sea, running water, and the sun. The last three plagues allude to historical and political events that were occurring or were expected to occur soon. The seventh plague is identical to the other two in the series, a look to the future and events yet to come. Ever since the days of the Exodus, oppressed people have found a liberating power to guide them through the calamities of history. After the pain and struggle, liberty and happiness await in the future. The wicked, who live in darkness and have nothing to look forward to, feel desperate and lost. The plagues that were calls to conversion become for them part of their torture.

49.

What is the Armageddon (Rv 16:16)? When will it occur?

Literally, Armageddon means "Mountain of Megiddo." Megiddo was a fortified city north of Israel, close to Mount Carmel. It guarded the entrance to the plain of Esdraelon, the principal source of grain for the country.

Because of its strategic location, Megiddo had been the battleground for some of the most decisive battles in Jewish history. Archeological excavations have uncovered evidence that the city was destroyed some thirty times in wars fought in the region (see Jgs 5:19; 2 Kgs 9:27; 23:29; 2 Chr 35:22). Megiddo is where, in Judges 5, Deborah and Barak triumphed over Sisera; where, in 2 Kings 9, King Jehu of Israel and King Ahaziah of Judah battled each other. Megiddo became a sad chapter in the history of Israel as a result of those events and, even more so, because of the defeat and death of King Josiah at the hands of King Neco of Egypt. Because of those battles where the fate of Israel was at stake, Armageddon becomes the apocalyptic battleground for the forces of good and evil, which will be driven by God to their destruction.

There are some scholars who say that the Armageddon of Revelation alludes to the "mount of assembly" (Is 14:13), a campground and staging area for the forces of evil who battle the armies of the faithful camped on Mount Zion (see Rv 14:1). The evil powers will never harm those protected by God.

A few present-day commentators see the coming of Armageddon in the wars and strife occurring throughout the countries of the Middle East. Fundamentalists who think the end of the world is near do not doubt the imminence of the "final battle."

The author of Revelation was not thinking about events that would take place 2,000 years after his time, but about the conditions of his period and the developments that were expected to unfold soon. He used the symbolic language of the Old Testament. The author was looking to the defeat of the forces of evil, which he saw incarnated in the Roman Empire which persecuted Christians. Armageddon historically occurs every time the forces of evil are defeated by the power of faith. When the armies of evil join forces and become an oppressive threat, Christians must pray for their Armageddon.

50.

Why is Rome called the great harlot or prostitute (Rv 17:1-7)? Does this title refer to the Roman Catholic Church?

The author of Revelation was thinking of the challenges and persecutions facing his Christian readers, especially the persecution by the Roman Empire, which worked to implant their imperial cult beliefs on conquered peoples. In biblical language, the term "prostitution" has a religious meaning; the relationship between God and his People (Israel) and humankind is compared to a marriage. Thus, idolatry is a form of adultery or religious prostitution. When the prophets stated that all the Israelites were adulterers, they were not thinking of them as women-chasers, but of Israelites who were in pursuit of Baal, a false God. The Roman Empire, in attempting to impose its imperial religion on conquered nations, was driving them into religious prostitution.

To the author of Revelation, Rome was the embodiment of all the evil that had historically afflicted the new People of God, the Christian community; it was a new Babylon, Nineveh, and Sodom. In chapter twelve, the author offers a vision of the woman—the Church—pursued by the dragon. The "Great Harlot" is the anti-woman and anti-church. The Church is the virgin, the wife of the Lamb, and her enemy is the harlot wife of Satan.

The harlot of the Book of Revelation rides on the beast like a goddess on horseback, supported and sustained by the beast. She is wearing purple and scarlet, symbolizing the luxury and ostentation that blanketed the spiritual emptiness of the Roman Empire. The prostitutes of Rome, like this harlot, were accustomed to wearing a diadem on their foreheads with their names or symbol. Many say that the description of the harlot contains elements that in the Book of Exodus are attributed to the sanctuary of God and the vestments of the high priest. Because of this, they say, the harlot is a blasphemous parody of everything that is divine (see Ex 25:3-7; 26:1,31,36; 27:16; 28:5,15,23).

The name of this woman is *mystery* because her title does not refer to Babylon in the literal sense but to Rome (Rv 17:5). In several ancient Greek manuscripts the title of the woman appears in capital letters: "Babylon the great, mother of whores and of earth's abominations" (17:5). In all probability, early readers saw in the title a numerical value whose meaning is unknown to us.

The presentation of the city of Rome and the Roman Empire in the figure of a prostitute probably was very significant to Christian readers of the latter part of the first century. The Roman authors Juvenal (A.D. 110-130) and Tacitus (circa A.D. 150) wrote about the famous Roman Empress Messalina, wife of Emperor Claudius, who reigned in the middle of the first century. Messalina truly was a prostitute whose life was so scandalous that her husband had her executed. In the eyes of Christians, Messalina was a symbol of total Roman corruption and decay in her city.

Some Protestant denominations like to identify the harlot of Revelation with the Roman Catholic Church. This identification is gross blasphemy. The author describes the harlot as the power of evil that threatens all saints. The Catholic Church, notwithstanding its human defects, struggles for justice and well-being in the world. It is anti-evangelical to denigrate her with false accusations.

In line with the thoughts of the author, we should ask where the harlot lives today and how she succeeds in turning nations into religious prostitutes, away from God and away from the values of the gospel, and how she persecutes those who seek justice. Maybe the harlot lives in luxury in many places in the world, but she certainly doesn't live among the poor of the world. In ancient times, the harlot incited to idolatry of the imperial cult; today she incites to idolatry of wealth and materialism.

51

Who are the seven kings represented by the seven heads of the great harlot of the Book of Revelation (17:9-14)?

John constantly alludes to the situation of Christians living in the Roman Empire. The enumeration and description of the kings help us understand something of the chronology of the book. The author introduced the seven heads with a call to reflect: "This calls for a mind that has wisdom" (Rv 17:9). Here, as in other places in the text where similar passages are found, the author wanted his readers to realize that he spoke of things happening all around them; he was talking about Rome and the governing emperors (see 12:10.18).

The author suggests that he writes during the reign of the sixth emperor: "They are seven kings, of whom five have fallen, one is living, and the other has not yet come" (Rv 17:9-10). Then he announces that the king who is yet to come will reign for a short time; after which the author surprises the reader by adding that there is an eighth king who is the beast—and who is, in fact, one of the seven.

In all probability, the author was thinking of the emperors Nero and Domitian, who were responsible for the first persecutions of Christians. The emperor who was to come and reign for a short time would have been Tito, who ruled for just two years. Like we said when talking about the beast, Domitian was the new Nero and a beast of a man. Even pagan writers bring up the similarity between the two emperors in their madness and inhumanity.

The list of the first eight emperors with their respective reigns will help better understand what the author of Revelation is talking about:

     1. Augustus   31 B.C. - A.D. 14
     2. Tiberius   A.D. 14-37

3. Caligula   A.D. 37-41
4. Claudius   A.D. 41-54
5. Nero   A.D. 54-68
Between A.D. 68 and 69, Galba, Oton, and Vitelius fought each other in a civil war for control of the Empire. None was able to assume power.
6. Vespasian   A.D. 69-79
7. Tito   A.D. 79-81
8. Domitian   A.D. 81-96

In reality, it is probable that the author of Revelation wrote in the time of Domitian and had, in his imagination, established himself in the period of Nero's rule in order to write about his visions. And there are some who think that the beast quite possibly could be Vespasian "who was" the favorite of Nero, then lost his favor—"is no more"—and who would rise again to take control of the empire. But, as we said above, the beast in all probability was Emperor Nero.

52.

How will Rome and the forces of evil be destroyed (Rv 17:15; 18:24)? Will there be a miraculous intervention by God in the final act of history?

In the Book of Revelation Rome is a symbol and compendium of Satan's hostility toward the Church. As Jesus announced in the gospel, "The gates of Hades will not prevail against it" (Mt 16:18). We must bear in mind that chapter eighteen of Revelation is a poem, and we should not interpret it literally. The poem speaks of Rome as a goddess personified, as a city, and as an empire. Rome indeed fell, but not in the poetic manner described in Revelation. In describing the Roman collapse, the author was inspired by the destruction of reigns and cities described in the Old Testament—cities such as Jerusalem at the hands of the

Babylonians, Babylon at the hands of the Persians, the fall of the king of Tyre (see Ez 18), and the destruction of Sodom and Gomorrah. Just as sinners and enemies of God perished in ancient times, so will the evil powers of Rome perish, taking to its death an empire that considered itself omnipotent.

The Roman Empire crumbled away gradually from the inside; its external enemies only hastened its inevitable fall. Rome did not burn, but was plundered by the Visigoths; the tragedy could not be appreciated from the sea. The author dreams of the fall of Rome and sings dramatically with a lament similar to the grieving songs used in the tragedies of ancient times. The friends of Rome—kings, magnates, merchants, the wealthy, navigators, mariners—pronounce their verses of lament. Babylon/Rome will end like Jerusalem in the Lamentations of Jeremiah (see Jer 25:10).

Revelation underscores the contrast between the weeping and mourning on earth by the friends of Rome and the rejoicing in heaven. The cries of the rich and powerful will be answered by the happiness of the poor—saints, apostles, prophets—just as it had been announced in the Old Testament.

The fall of Babylon and the cities of sin are proof that the powers of evil shall not prevail in history. Christians have to accelerate the fall of these sinful communities with prayer and a commitment to kindness and justice. God does not bring an end to evil through spectacular miracles, but through the quiet yet effective action of his faithful. Christians cannot "marry" or reconcile with any social or political system that places material things ahead of the people; nor can they form a union with rulers who confer honors, power, and wealth on the privileged few. The New Jerusalem that Christians await and struggle for will be an island of peace and joy and love inviting all mankind to be part of it.

53.

Why was Rome so important to the author of the Book of Revelation?

When Revelation was written, Rome was the most important city in the world—at least from an administrative, political, military, and economic point of view. For Jews and for large numbers of Christians, Jerusalem remained the religious center of the world. For others, however, Athens was the cultural center from which radiated the true civilization destined to conquer minds and spirits.

Rome, with its laws and decrees, profoundly affected the lives of the first Christians. The persecution by Nero and the death of the apostles Peter and Paul had left an open wound in the hearts of many. The author of Revelation saw in Rome a nest of evil and of persecutors of Christians and of all who resisted their oppresive legions.

The Roman powers, like conquerors of other historical periods, considered themselves beneficent since they carried their civilization and culture into nations they controlled.

The author of Revelation did not want anyone to be deceived, and for this reason he denounced with clarity and directness the evils of the imperial system.

Rome was the home of the great harlot, the throne of the beast. We must, however, remember that the description offered in Revelation is of a prophetic nature. Until the arrival of the plenitude of the messianic kingdom, and until the celestial Jerusalem becomes a reality, the beast of the Book of Revelation will continue to occupy his thrones in many parts of the world. From those seats of sin will come the laws and decrees that oppress nations and oppose the Christian message of justice, respect, and universal love.

In the course of history, Christians will have to keep their eyes and ears open to guard against the propaganda and false values handed down from the headquarters of the beast. They will have to denounce them without fear.

54.

Who is the rider on the white horse in the Book of Revelation (19:11-13)?

The horseman that appears riding a white horse in chapter nineteen of Revelation is Christ glorious and triumphant as he descends from the heavens to eliminate forever the forces of evil. The glorious Christ makes real the "Day of the Lord," the Final Judgment that will liberate the faithful.

The description of the horseman is filled with symbolic details that make clear the power and glory of Christ triumphant. His internal qualities are described first: he is faithful; he is truthful; he is just. A physical description follows: eyes, head, mouth, and dress. His armies and the forces of victory follow him, mounted on white horses.

The Christ who appears for the Final Judgment is the Christ of Calvary, the glorious Christ, the triumphant Lamb who appeared before and now arrives for the Second Coming or Parousia. He will destroy forever the power of evil and restore the original glory of creation.

His personal name, "that no one knows except himself," is "the name that is above every name" (Phil 2:9). No one knows the name exactly, so it cannot be manipulated or controlled. And he has still another name, "King of kings and Lord of lords," which proclaims his greatness before all nations.

When Jesus came to earth for the first time, he came incognito; he arrived almost like a stranger, a foreigner, or an illegal alien: weak and humble. Only a few of the faithful recognized him, understood him, and believed in his work and in his victory. His Second Coming, however, is so magnificent that nobody can ignore him. Everybody must come face to face with he who was pierced in Calvary: the King of the world.

98

The rider on the white horse in chapter nineteen of Revelation is very different from the four horsemen who appeared at the opening of the first four seals (6:1-8). Those riders were messengers of misfortune, of plagues that fell upon all mankind to call people to convert. The rider on the white horse in the end comes to execute the judgment against those who refused to believe, and to bring the glory and the reward to his own followers.

The author of Revelation viewed with happiness and delight the triumph of Christ in his communities. His coming was gradually becoming a reality. The powers of evil and of the Roman Empire were destined to fail. Christians had united with a stronger army ready to win the final battle.

55.

What is the meaning of the title, "King of kings" and "Lord of lords" (Rv 19:16)?

This title proclaims that Jesus has received all the power in heaven and on earth (see Mt 28:16). In the ancient Greek small-letter manuscripts, the words for this title are written in capital letters, an indication that they symbolized something special.

The value of each letter (Hebrew) of the title totals 777, which is the perfect number repeated three times. This indicates that Jesus carries the perfect title of Conqueror of evil, or King of the Universe:

M L K		M L K Y N		M R '		M R W N	
40 30 20		40 30 20 10 50		40 200 1		40 200 6 50	
KING	(OF)	KINGS		LORD	(OF)	LORDS		
90	+	150	+	241	+	296 = 777		

The title "King of kings and Lord of lords" announces the universal lordship of Jesus resurrected. His title is probably written on his banner, not on his thigh. It's possible to confuse some translated words because of the similarity in the Hebrew terms thigh, *rgl,* and banner, *dgl.* Some may even think that the author was really referring to an equestrian statue that stood in Ephesus and whose rider had his name inscribed on his thigh. In any case, the thigh is the part of the body that is especially visible when a person is mounted on a horse.

56.

What is the millennium (Rv 20:1-6)? How will it occur?

At the end of Revelation, the triumph of Christ and Christians is described in detail. The author has repeatedly alluded to the final victory: Christ comes to earth to destroy the power of evil by incapacitating it for one thousand years. The martyrs will then reign with Christ for a thousand years, and at the end of that period the power of evil will rise again as a great force for a short time before its final destruction (Rv 20:14).

Many readers of Revelation ignore the author's manner and style of writing and interpret this section literally. They see the return of paradise-like conditions on earth, in such a way that the world will be at the end just like the Book of Genesis presented it in the beginning.

Millenarianism has encountered opposition from the Church since ancient times. The doctrine of the millennium, the so-called reign of Christ on earth with the elect, especially the martyrs, for 1,000 years, is a modification of the Jewish belief concerning the chosen People. These People would live in the ideal future and would dominate all other peoples and rule the world. Daniel talks about a messianic reign that will last forever (see Dan 7:14,27). The Apocalypse of Baruch also talks of an eternal messianic reign after the destruction of the powers of evil. The Sibylline Oracles (3:652ss) and the Apocalypse of Enoch (91:12ss) speak of an intermediate messianic reign before the final establishment of God's sovereignty over the world. According to Jewish tradition, the duration of the messianic reign varies from 400 to 7,000 years. In ancient Persian mythology there is frequent mention of an evil power that is chained for a thousand years. It was expected that during the millennium there would be an absence of evil and an abundance of material and spiritual good. The word *millenarianism*, a word derived from Latin, is also called *chiliasm*, a term derived from the Greek language. Millenarianism was proposed in different forms by some Fathers of the Church (Justin, Irenaeus, Hippolytus).

Saint Augustine offered a spiritualized interpretation of the millennium in line with the Gospel of John (Jn 5:24-29). John wrote of two resurrections: a spiritual one that takes place when a person believes in Jesus and begins a new life, and another resurrection at the end into glory with Jesus. In this respect, the texts of Revelation that address the first resurrection and the millennium should be understood in the context of the life of liberty and freedom enjoyed by the faithful. Christians have the joy of God in them; they feel secure, confident and have no fear. There is nothing that can enslave them, and they enjoy the liberty and the glory of Christ.

Some biblical specialists read the texts of Revelation dealing with the resurrection and the millennium in light of the resurrection of the dry bones described in the vision of Ezekiel. The prophet was announcing the resurrection of the people captive in Babylonia. To these specialists, John was referring to the "resurrection" and revitalization of the Church struggling to survive the death threats of Roman persecutors. The "thousand years" was probably referring to the life of freedom in the Church when the persecutions were ended. The Church continues to live the millennium. The number "1000" symbolizes plenitude, fullness of time, a very long and indeterminate period.

The general Catholic interpretation follows that of Saint

Augustine. The "thousand years" do not refer to a chronology of events, but have a theological meaning. It is a period of the glory of the new creation, starting with the triumph of Christ. As Christians, we now live the glory of Christ as the author wrote in his Letter to the Hebrews:

"But, you have come to Mount Zion and the city of the living God, the heavenly Jerusalem, and to the innumerable angels in festal gathering, and the assembly of the firstborn who are enrolled in heaven, and God the judge of all, and to the spirits of the righteous made perfect, and to Jesus, the mediator of a new covenant, and to the sprinkled blood that speaks a better word than the blood of Abel" (Heb 12:22-24).

The author of Revelation believed that the powers of evil could remain victorious only for a brief period of three and one-half years. The forces of good, on the other hand, could triumph for one thousand years, symbolically meaning a long, indefinite period.

Throughout its history, the Church has dealt with errors regarding the millennium. Catholics, however, have consistently rejected—from the third ecumenical Council of Ephesus in A.D. 431, through the Middle Ages, to modern times—literal and materialistic interpretations that don't take into consideration the mind of the author who wrote the book.

Abbot Joachim de Fiore taught that the millennium would begin in the year 1260. In modern times, Mormons, Dispensationalists, Adventists, Jehovah's Witnesses, and other groups have erroneously taught their own variations of millenarianism; they await a physical and material reign of the just on earth before the Final Judgment.

57

Who are Gog and Magog (Rv 20:7-10)? What do they represent?

Gog and Magog are two names that appear in the Book of Ezekiel. Gog is King of Magog; Magog is a mythical place situated north of Asia Minor in the confines of the Black Sea. In the apocalyptic books, Gog and Magog are a formula to describe the powers working against God (see Sib.Orac 3,2319.512; 4 Esdr 13,5ss; Apoc of Enoch 56,5ss). Readers may get the impression that the two names refer to persons, especially when examining the visionary writings of the prophets.

Ezekiel refers to the apocalyptic enemies of the People of God, a symbol of all the enemies destined to be destroyed by God in order that his People may live in freedom. In Revelation, Gog and Magog represent the incredulous pagan nations that oppose the Church, the new People of God, in the final days of the world.

The end-of-the-world battle presented in this section compares to the visionary assault described in chapter nineteen of Revelation. In both cases the power of evil is rendered absolutely impotent and is defeated without any resistance. Satan, who no longer has the beasts at his command, forms an alliance with political powers and together they attack the saints.

John did not expect that the defeat of the Roman Empire would bring an end to the problems plaguing Christians. Time after time the devil will raise his ugly head, but he is condemned to fail.

58

How will the Final Judgment occur (Rv 19:11–20:15)?

All the biblical texts that talk about the Final Judgment are written in an apocalyptic style, with descriptions full of traditional symbolism taken from the prophets and from Exodus. Historically, these books refer to the judgment and defeat of the pagan nations enemies of the People of God. History is replete with God's judgments.

The Final Judgment was announced in Revelation 14:14-20 with the double-image of reaping and vintage. The reaping appears to affect the faithful, the grain that is gathered in God's granaries; the vintage affects the unfaithful who become the object of God's ire.

The judgment is narrated in detail in Revelation (19:11-20:15). The judgment is the definitive triumph of Christ and Christians, a full-blown victory of the faithful over the impotence of evil. This judgment is occurring throughout history. The author of Revelation uses the vocabulary of prophet Daniel (see Dan 7:9-14). In Daniel, as in Paul (1 Cor 15:25) and Revelation, the last enemy to be defeated is death. The powers of death must be defeated by Christians throughout history. The decisive victory will come with God.

The Final Judgment is frequently imagined along the lines described by Matthew (25:31-46). Modern biblical commentators refer to it as the "parable" of the Final Judgment. One cannot imagine an unnumerable multitude gathered in the valley of Josafat, made up of people who do not know whether they are going to heaven or hell.

Matthew spoke of the Christian community as being the entrance into the kingdom. Throughout history, final events are taking place. The decisions people make for Christ and for the poor (the hungry, the naked, the sick, and so forth) have eternal dimensions and consequences.

Life is full of opportunities. Christ is always at the door, waiting to be let in. Every failure is a kind of end of the world: when a loved one dies, when an economic breakdown occurs, when one's reputation is lost, the world ends for a person. At that moment Christ is at the door to offer a new hope; a new world will open; a new life will begin.

59.

Will the Rapture really happen? Will the faithful be "caught up" to meet the Lord in heaven? What is the Catholic view of this?

The Rapture is one of the principal doctrines of many evangelical and fundamentalist denominations. Although the doctrine is proposed in different forms by the diverse denominations, certain elements are held in common by all these groups. According to this doctrine, the souls or spirits of the elect who are alive in the last days will be "caught up" together with the dead to meet the Lord in paradise and will escape the evils that come upon the world. At the end, those who are raptured will form Christ's court when he comes to judge and reign over the world for a thousand years. During those thousand years the world will have the order and rectitude that God wanted for his creation since the beginning, but which had been subverted by the temptation and the fall of Adam and Eve.

This so-called Rapture is not mentioned in Revelation. Fundamentalists and evangelicals, however, make it a part of this book in the context of the final battle that will destroy the wicked. The theory of the Rapture is derived from the following sections of the Bible: Mark 13:27; Matthew 24:31,40-41; 1 Thessalonians 4:13ss; Revelation 20.

Many people believe that the Rapture will actually occur, just as Paul describes it in his letter to the Thessalonians: the elect, those who are alive and follow Christ, will be caught up in the air with Christ, and they will become transformed into spiritual beings clothed with immortality. This should occur seven years before the coming of the millennium when Christ will come again with his saints to engage the wicked enemy and win the final battle.

The seven years between the Rapture and the millennium will be years of great tribulation, in that all good values and all true Christian influence will have been taken from this world. The sermons and lectures about Jesus will continue, especially for those persons who were not totally prepared for the Rapture; the preachers, however, will not be heard nor will they have any effect on society. In those years, wickedness and sin will prevail.

The doctrine of the Rapture, which is also found in apocryphal books (see 1 Enoch 39:3-4; 2 Enoch 7), comes from an arbitrary and poor interpretation of the texts of holy Scripture. The number "seven" and the "great tribulation" have a symbolic significance in the Bible. The "two persons; one will be taken, and one will be left" in Matthew refers to the mystery of the conversion, as well as the acceptance of the gospel which mysteriously occurs by the grace of God (24:40-41). The language of Paul was filled with allusions to his mystic experiences. In addition, he used the symbols of his his time reserved for the coming or arrival of the emperor in the city or region. This language cannot be taken literally to apply to Christ because he is above all human conceptual forms and surpasses all human values.

The doctrine of the Rapture, like that of the millennium, has never been accepted in the Catholic Church. The Rapture implies a literal, materialized, or materialistic interpretation of spiritual realities.

Most Protestant denominations have also rejected the doctrine of the Rapture. Still, in most Christian circles, a tiny nucleus can be found that continues to dream of it.

60

What is the vision
of the New Jerusalem (Rv 21:5-27)?

The author of Revelation visualized the New Jerusalem from all angles, inside and out. In chapter twenty-one of Revelation he described the exterior of the city as a bride in gleaming splendor, a faithful virgin—everything about her contrary to the great Roman harlot described in chapter seventeen. Her twelve gates and twelve layers of foundation represent the unity of the two covenants of the tribes of Israel; together with the twelve apostles of the Church, they form the one People of God.

The city is shaped like a great cube, fifteen hundred miles in length, width, and height. The wall measures one hundred and forty-four cubits. The size of the wall does not appear to be proportionate in relation to the other dimensions of the city and probably serves as adornment more than a defensive structure. The wall is protected by God himself and represents the unity of all its inhabitants.

The description of the interior of the city (Rv 21:22-22:5) indicates that it does not have a sanctuary or Temple of God, because the entire city is one great temple. The author appears to be somewhat surprised at the absence of the Temple because his narrow Jewish nationalism clashes with Christian universalism.

God is the light and the salvation of the city. His city is a place of open doors, inviting everyone to abandon a world of sin and false values to become a part of the community of God. The city is the new paradise, and the center is occupied by God and the Lamb.

The author mentioned the ideal position of the Christian community in the world inviting all nations to conversion. The City of God is the alternative to the city of Babylon, of the beast. Babylon is destined to fail, wheras the City of God is the key to the future of the Church and the world. As a traditional Spanish song says, "We are a pilgrim people until; we shall walk until we reach the city that never ends, free from grief and sorrow, a city for eternity."

61.

How is the new paradise described in the book of Revelation (22:1-5)?

The author of Revelation describes the new paradise associated with the New Jerusalem and the ideal Church. The new community is described with sketches of paradise (rivers, trees) and with the liturgical elements (throne, temple, cult). The new paradise, like the original described in Genesis, is a symbolic place—a place of peace, joy, and good fortune.

Paradise is all-inclusive in the history of salvation, appearing at the beginning and at the end; all events in history point toward a new creation. God, who had spoken at the beginning of creation, saying, "Let there be light," speaks at the end, saying, "I am making all things new," and, "It is done!" (Rv 21:5-6). The final and perfect creation is a reality.

John was inspired by Genesis and by Ezekiel 47:1-12. The new paradise, like the new creation, surpasses the original garden in not having a tree whose fruit was forbidden to eat. Instead, it has an avenue lined with trees of life that produce fruits of immortality. The paradise described is nostalgic and filled with hope for Christians.

Jesus has opened the gates of paradise for us ever since he came. It's possible to live together, to have true peace and harmony. We receive the medicines of immortality (sacraments), and God walks with us throughout our existence. The sea exists no more—storms, agitation, uncertainty, fear, danger, anxieties, and disorder. In the new paradise there is only rest and peace.

The "spring of the water of life" is much more abundant

than the "fountain" that watered the first paradise (Rv 21:6). The People of God in the Old Testament awaited that water, and believed it would come in messianic times. Jesus identified the water of life with his doctrine and with the Holy Spirit. These are communicated to the faithful who participate in the life of the Church.

62.

What is the meaning of the final expression in the Book of Revelation, *Marana tha* (22:17)?

Marana tha, "Our Lord has come!," is an expression that also appears in 1 Corinthians 16:22 and in other parts of the New Testament. *Marana tha* are two words from the Aramaic language which form a part of the liturgical language used by the first Christians. The words originally expressed the impatience and fervent hope for a Parousia in which the glorious lordship of Jesus over all creation would be revealed.

Marana tha also expresses the indomitable optimism of communities under constant persecution by the powers of the empire. They knew that the evil enemy would not last forever. The triumph of Christ and Christians would soon become a reality. This encouraged them to persevere and to continue to resist. The author of Revelation attempted to nourish the faith and stimulate the enthusiasm that made Christians exclaim, *"Marana tha."*

Also by Juan Alfaro...for Spanish readers

Introducción a la Biblia
101 Preguntas y Respuestas
Originally published in Mexico, *Introducción a la Biblia* is a collection of probing questions about the Bible that many people have posed to the author. The answers provided are written in simple language. $5.95

More resources from Liguori...

Catholic Answers to Fundamentalists' Questions
by Philip St. Romain
St. Romain offers clear, accurate information on basic areas of faith and practice: Scripture and tradition, salvation, devotions to Mary and the saints, and more. $2.95
Also available in Spanish...Respuestas Católicas a Preguntas Fundamentalistas. $2.95

Catholic Answers to Questions About the New Age Movement
by Ronald Quillo; Foreword by Philip St. Romain
Inspired by the teachings of the Bible, the Church, and the New Age movement itself, Quillo provides information on a Catholic position regarding the New Age movement, with practical guidelines for daily faith life. $2.95

Catholic Answers to Contemporary Questions
by Daniel L. Lowery, C.SS.R.
This book answers questions about faith issues such as the Mass, prayer, purgatory, and sin. It also discusses some of today's controversial moral questions concerning vital issues like euthanasia, living wills, and AIDS. $2.95

Order from your local bookstore or write to
Liguori Publications
Box 060, Liguori, MO 63057–9999
(Please add $2 for postage and handling to orders under $10;
$3 for orders between $10 and $15; $4 for orders over $15.)